Frank's
Old World Secrets
To Good Italian Cooking

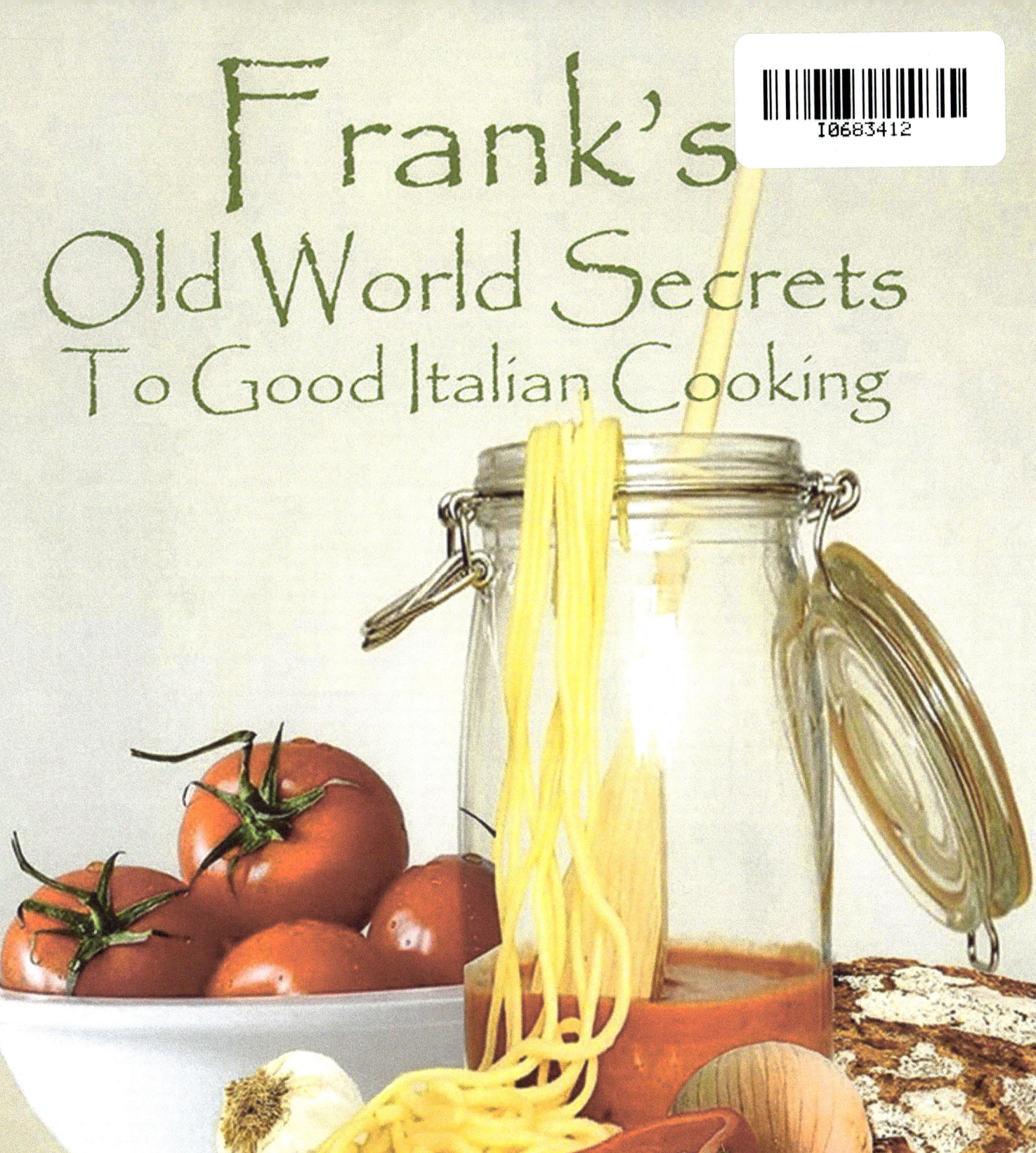

Frank's
Old World Secrets
To Good Italian Cooking

Chef Frank Renda

CITI OF
BOOKS

CITIOFBOOKS, INC.
3736 Eubank NE Suite A1
Albuquerque, NM 87111-3579
www.citiofbooks.com
Hotline: 1 (877) 389-2759
Fax: 1 (505) 930-7244

Ordering Information:

Quantity sales. Special discounts are available on quantity purchases by corporations, associations, and others. For details, contact the publisher at the address above.

Printed in the United States of America.

ISBN-13:   Softcover   979-8-89391-310-1
               eBook   979-8-89391-311-8
               Hardback   979-8-89391-330-9

Library of Congress Control Number: 2024918444

I was born in Ragusa, Italy, in the fifties (what a great day). At the young age of three, I came to America with my parents and grew up in Jersey City, NJ. My father was a barber with his own shop. My mom was the chief cook and bottle washer. She would always serve my father and me hand and foot. Okay, yes. I was spoiled. She would prepare great Italian dishes. All I wanted was pasta and steak and nothing else. Again, I was spoiled.

Well, that all changed with our first trip to Italy, when I was eight. I needed to expand my palate. I had to let new ingredients into my life. I realized there was a new world of food—great food such as cheeses, sauces, meats, chicken and, yes, fish. Oh my God, eight years wasted on pasta and steak only. There were salads with fresh tomatoes, potatoes and, yes, food that swam in the ocean—clams, mussels, shrimp, lobster, calamari, etc. Then there were vegetables (no thanks). Guess what? There were also peppers and onions, asparagus, broccoli, rapini, spinach, cabbage...wait, they have this vegetable called escarole? What the.... Then I was introduced to fagiolini beans. Can you believe that? Beans, zucchini, and then there was melanzane (eggplant). Then, if my heart couldn't take any more, there was Italian pizza—pizza that you eat with a knife and fork. Can you believe that? A knife and fork to eat pizza! I would go to bed at night with a smile on my face and love in my tummy. I couldn't wait to see what wonderful food I would eat the next day! I felt I was reborn to a world of delight and amazement. Finally I discovered gelato; espresso and dolce (desserts); torta di ricotta (cheesecake), which was to die for; zeppole Di Sangiuseppe; struffoli; cannoli; spumoni; brutti ma buoni (ugly but good nut cookies); and biscotti. Then on my third trip to Italy, at the age of sixteen, I was introduced to Italian wines. And that's a whole other story....

When I returned to the U.S.A., I had a whole new outlook on food and its preparations. I looked for better-quality foods, wine, and pairing.

Then I meet my wife, Lucinda, a great cook. I'm talking a gourmet cook! She also spoiled me with her Italian dishes (she picked up where my mom left off). Between my wife and mom, I didn't need to even boil water. Don't forget, I was spoiled. Well, for many years, we enjoyed the best of Italian food at home and out. Then my life and Lucinda's life ran into a major crossroad. Lucinda, my "dolce vita," developed a major spinal disorder, for which there is no cure, just heavy medication, and shortly after I became ill. Once I finally recovered, I was faced with the fact that my wife was unable to perform her kitchen magic. At that point, I decided to take over the house and kitchen duties. Now it was my turn to spoil others.

I would like to explain that in my whole life, I would always observe all of the special techniques that were being used by great cooks in my family, but I was searching for the secret to good Italian cooking. What is the secret ingredient? This is the question for all! I of all people finally discovered the answer. It comes in multi-parts. The main secret is "LOVE." You must love and be excited to cook in the kitchen and be able to create a special dish. The passion! The other part of the answer is to use *only* fresh ingredients, such as fresh garlic, parsley, onions, lemons, sea salt, fresh-ground pepper, rosemary, meats, chicken, and fish. As long as you use these fresh ingredients, you'll never create a bad dish or meal. Never be afraid to experiment and create your own dishes, as I have done.

Now let me share with you some of my famous recipes that I have created. Remember, love, fresh ingredients, and preparation equal great food. Have fun!

P.S. If you really love these recipes, please let me know. I'll write another book and share more with you!

P.S.S. As of today, I lost my wife and have been blessed and have another soulmate to share my life with.

frankjosephrenda@gmail.com

I wrote this book to share the love I have for good Italian cooking and the old world secrets, to share my experiences and travels throughout Italy and Sicily. The secret recipes of my relatives and acquaintances that I have found in the old country were the best of the best which create the magic of Italian foods. The way that ingredients are paired together and how they automatically are attracted to your senses the smell, the sight and most of all the reward you get from the taste. As you follow me in my creations you too will experience the same. Most of all I will give you the ability to do the same and become an Italian chef. Then you'll have the greatest feeling watching your guests enjoy your Italian food that you have created! Enjoy!

Dedication

I am dedicating this cook book to Lucinda, my wife, my best friend, my reason for living. I would like to thank you for your inspirational talks and mostly in your belief in my abilities to create Italian food dishes. Mostly for your loving words and affection to me to follow this dream in writing and expressing my hidden abilities for Italian Cooking.

RECIPES

FRANK'S SPAGHETTI AGLIO E' OLIO

(Spaghetti, Garlic, and Oil)

Ingredients:
Sea salt and fresh-ground mill pepper (to taste)
½ cup fresh minced garlic (10 cloves)
¾ cup Italian extra virgin oil (evoo)
6 tablespoons fresh chopped Italian flat-leaf parsley
1 pound spaghetti or linguine, your pick
1 tablespoon anchovy paste or 4 fillets minced anchovies
½ teaspoon crushed red pepper flakes (optional: If you don't like spicy, just use ground pepper)
1½ cups grated Pecorino-Romano cheese (add more if needed)
1 cup toasted Italian seasoned breadcrumbs

Directions:
In a large pot, add 4 to 6 qts of water and bring to boil, then add ¼ cup sea salt. Add your pasta of choice and cook for 8 to 9 minutes until al dente or longer if you desire softer.

In the meantime, in a large sauté pan or skillet, heat up evoo on medium heat and sauté the garlic and anchovies, along with the pepper flakes, to light golden color (do not burn the garlic. If so start over. Burnt garlic gives everything a bad taste). Once your pasta is ready, drain and add to your sauté mixture and stir for 30 seconds. Shut off the burner and add your grated cheese and breadcrumbs. Add some pasta water if too dry but not too much. Stir, plate, and serve.

You can make this dish without the grated cheese and toasted breadcrumbs. I sometimes do, and it's great.

MIO ZUPPA DI MINESTRONE

(My Minestrone Soup)

Ingredients:
4-6 cups chopped cabbage
¼ cup minced fresh garlic
¾ cup Italian extra virgin olive oil (evoo)
3-4 cups diced zucchini squash
4 large potatoes, peeled and diced
4 stalks clean celery, diced
3 cups diced white sweet onion
3 cups cannellini beans (soaked in water overnight)
3 cups red kidney beans (soaked in water overnight)
4 carrots, cleaned and diced
5-6 cups Tuttorossi (diced tomatoes) with the juices
10 cups College Inn culinary broth, white wine, and herbs
3 tablespoons fresh chopped Italian basil
2 tablespoons fresh chopped sage
½ cup fresh chopped Italian flat-leaf parsley
¾-1 pound pancetta or good bacon
1 pound any mini-pasta shells or broken spaghetti (1-inch pieces)
Kosher salt and fresh-ground mill pepper (always to taste)

Directions:
In a large sauté pan, add evoo. Heat on medium heat. Sauté onion, garlic, and pancetta until tender (be careful not to burn the garlic. If so start over). Add tomatoes with juice and all vegetables and simmer for 15 minutes, adding salt and fresh-ground pepper to taste (add 2 tablespoons of sugar, which cuts the acid in the tomatoes). While it is simmering in a large deep pot on medium heat, add the culinary broth and 2 cups of water. Stir and after 2 minutes, add all of your sauté from the sauté pan and bring to a boil. Add your herbs and your drained beans. Stir for 3 minutes and turn down the heat to a simmer for 45 minutes with a lid on the pot. Then add your pasta and salt and pepper to taste. Cook for 10 minutes. Add water if soup seems too thick. Cook until pasta is tender and soup is steamy. Remove and serve in bowls. You can also sprinkle with your favorite grated cheese to taste and just enjoy.

CIOPPINO CON MERLUZZO

(Fish Soup)

Ingredients:
2 pounds merluzzo (favorite whitefish)
1½ dozen fresh cleaned mussels
1½ dozen fresh cleaned littleneck clams
1½ dozen fresh cleaned and peeled shrimp with veins removed (size is optional)
5 stalks cleaned celery, diced
¾ cup Italian extra virgin olive oil (evoo)
3-4 cups Tuttorossi diced tomatoes (can use Hunt's brand also)
8 cups College Inn culinary broth (white wine and herbs)
2 tablespoons fresh minced garlic
¼-½ tablespoons fresh chopped Italian flat-leaf parsley
2 cups good Italian dry white wine
2 cups fresh sweet white onion, diced
½ stick salted butter
Sea salt and fresh-ground mill pepper
⅛ teaspoon saffron (very expensive but worth it)

Directions:
In a large pot on medium heat, add evoo and butter and heat for 2 minutes until butter is melted. Then start to sauté the onions and celery for 2-3 minutes until onions become translucent. Now add garlic and stir until light golden color (careful! Do not cook too long, as it will burn and you must start over). Then add the diced tomatoes with juices and simmer for 15 minutes (add a few tablespoons sugar for the acidity). Stir and add the culinary broth and wine and 1 to 2 cups of water, bringing to a boil. Once boiled, add the saffron and parsley. Season with salt and pepper to taste. Bring to a simmer for 30 minutes or longer. Then add your clams and mussels. Stir and cover for 15-20 minutes until clams and mussels are all open. Once open, add your merluzzo (whitefish choice) in small pieces, stir, and cook for five minutes, and then add your shrimp last. Cover and cook for 7 minutes until shrimp is pink in color. Remove from stovetop, place in a large deep bowl, and serve right out of the pot (why dirty another bowl, family style?), along with crusty Italian bread. Eat and dip and enjoy!

ZUPPE DI PASTA E' FAGIOLI

(Pasta and Bean Soup)

Ingredients:
1 large chopped fresh white sweet onion
3 stalks cleaned and chopped celery
3 tablespoons fresh minced garlic
½ cup Italian extra virgin olive oil (evoo)
¾ pound garbanzo beans (soaked in water overnight)
¾ pound cannellini beans (soaked in water overnight)
2 pounds fresh ripe tomatoes, diced with juices
1 tablespoon oregano, minced (you can use dry flakes)
2-3 bay leaves
1 tablespoon sea salt
1 tablespoon fresh-ground pepper
5 cups College Inn culinary broth (white wine and herbs)
1 pound your favorite pasta (if spaghetti, break into small pieces)

Directions:
In a large pot, combine your drained beans, put in pot, cover with water just to the top of beans, and bring to a boil. Then lower to a simmer for 45-60 minutes with lid on. Stir and check for dryness. Add a little water if needed until beans have a slightly tender feel. Now remove the lid and add your onion, garlic, celery, tomatoes with juices, culinary broth, and water (if needed), and bring to a boil. Once boiled, add oregano, salt and pepper to taste, and bay leaves. Stir well and lower heat to a simmer with the lid for an hour or so until all feels tender, then add your pasta. Stir and cook until pasta is to your liking. Then remove from stovetop with lid, let simmer for 10-15 minutes, then open and serve.

FRANK'S STUFFED ARTICHOKES

Ingredients:
4-6 large fresh artichokes
5 cups Italian seasoned breadcrumbs
4 eggs
1½ cups fresh grated Pecorine-Romano cheese
¾ cups fresh chopped Italian flat-leaf parsley
¼ cup fresh minced garlic
1 cup Italian extra virgin olive oil (evoo)
1½ teaspoons fresh-ground mill pepper
1½ teaspoons kosher or sea salt
32 oz College Inn culinary broth (white wine and herbs)
1 stick salted butter

Directions:
In an extra-large bowl, pour in breadcrumbs, cheese, parsley, garlic, salt, and pepper, and mix all together well. Then make a well in the center. Pour in evoo, eggs, and water, and mix all together until mixture becomes crumbly and not too sticky (if so just add a little more of the breadcrumbs). Now place your mixture aside. Take each artichoke and remove 2-3 layers of leaves all around. Now cut the bottoms of the stems flat off so the artichokes can stand upright. Place each artichoke in cold water with a few slices of lemon wedges (they keep them from turning brown). Remove each artichoke one at a time and shake dry. With a sharp bread knife, cut off all of the top pointy tips straight across, creating a flat surface on top. On a paper towel, place the tops upside down to drain any excess water just for a few minutes. Now take your bowl and create a deep well in the center to place your artichokes. Take each artichoke one at a time and bang the top of the artichoke against a hard surface (counter top or side of your sink) but not too hard so as not to break the artichoke, just to let the leaves spread out some. Now with your fingers, carefully spread the leaves apart but not too much, just so you can apply your stuffing mixture thoroughly throughout the whole artichoke, filling every cavity as much as possible.

Place each stuffed artichoke in a deep large Dutch oven pot, staying upright. Now pour in your culinary broth. Cover the artichokes about a quarter of the way up (do not cover the artichoke to the top with the broth, just a quarter). Put on medium heat and pour some evoo on top of each artichoke (about 1 tablespoon each while cooking). Cover with lid and check from time to time that the broth is about quarter of the way up the arti-choke (add as needed). Now bring to a low boil and, keeping broth level up, add pats of butter on top of each artichoke and baste each artichoke over and over with the hot broth, keeping them moist. Now let simmer and baste for about 60 minutes. Now you still need to add butter to the top of each artichoke and let melt in along with the basting. When time is up, test the leaves for tenderness. If soft, they're done. If not keep simmering until they are soft to touch. Once done, remove and place in a large bowl, along with some broth. Peel each leaf, place gently, with your teeth, pull off the meaty part of the inside leaf, placing the remaining leaf in an empty dish. Once you reach the bottom center of the artichoke with a knife, slice a thin layer of the artichoke's hair-like part off and just eat that meaty bottom part. It is just delicious.

CHICKEN PICCATA WITH LEMON CAPER SAUCE

Ingredients:

16 chicken breast, about 1/4 to1/2 inch thick

1½ cups fresh-squeezed lemon juice

1 stick salted butter

1-2 cups all-purpose flour

¼ cup fresh grated Pecorino-Romano cheese

1½ cups College Inn culinary broth (white wine and herb)

One jar drained capers (can use two jars)

¼ cup good Marsala wine

Kosher salt and fresh-ground pepper

½ cup Italian extra virgin olive oil (evoo)

3 tablespoons fresh chopped Italian flat-leaf parsley

3 beaten eggs with 3 tablespoons of milk or water (eggwash)

Directions:

On a hard surface, place a piece of wax paper or clear wrap. Place the chicken breasts on the surface and cover with another sheet. Pound each breast as thin as possible without breaking the meat. Then lightly salt and pepper each side and place on a large mixing tray or foil paper. Mix well together the flour and grated cheese, coating both sides and shaking off the excess, and dip in eggwash. In a large deep-frying pan or skillet heat on medium to high, add evoo and ½ stick of butter until melted. Then carefully place your coated chicken breasts using cooking tongs and not overcrowding the pan. Lightly brown each side. Place them on a warm platter and cover with foil. In the same pan, add the butter, lemon juice, capers, Marsala wine, and the broth, stirring and reducing to half. Then add your parsley. Check for taste on salt and pepper and add if needed. Then add your cooked chicken breasts. Cover, turn once, and simmer for 8-10 minutes. Place on hot plate, pour sauce over each breast, and enjoy.

VEAL PICCATA WITH MUSHROOMS

Ingredients:
10-14 veal fillets, about ¼-inch thick or less
1 cup fresh-squeezed lemon juice
1 stick salted butter
1-2 cups all-purpose flour
⅛ cup fresh grated Pecorino-Romano cheese
1½ cups College Inn culinary broth (white wine and herb)
Kosher salt and fresh-ground mill pepper
1 small jar drained capers
2 tablespoons Italian flat-leaf parsley, chopped
¼-½ cup Italian extra virgin olive oil (evoo)
1-2 cups fresh sliced mushrooms of choice (I prefer Portobello)
3 beaten eggs with 3 tablespoons of milk or water (eggwash)

Directions:
Take wax paper or clear wrap and place on a hard surface. Take each veal fillet and cover with another piece of wrap, then lightly pound each one to a thin size, careful not to break the meat. Now lightly salt and pepper each veal fillet (scallop). On a mixing tray or foil sheet, mix your flour and cheese together well and dust each veal fillet, and dip in egg wash. Now in a large frying pan or skillet on medium heat, add your evoo and ½ stick of butter. Once melted, quickly and lightly brown each veal fillet on each side (do not overcrowd the pan). Transfer to a warm platter and cover to keep warm. In the same pan/skillet, add some evoo if needed but not too much. Then add 1 to 2 tablespoons of butter, lemon juice, culinary broth, mushrooms, capers, and parsley. On medium heat, stir your sauce mixture and slowly reduce heat. Add your veal fillets, cook, and turn over each, spooning your sauce over each fillet for about 8 minutes. Quickly plate, serve hot with crusty Italian bread, and enjoy!

VEAL SHANKS OR CHOPS
WITH LEMON AND MUSHROOM SAUCE

Ingredients:

8 veal shanks roughly 1 inch thick (you can also with lamb chops)

5 tablespoons Italian extra virgin olive oil (evoo)

½ cup fresh-squeezed lemon juice

½ stick salted butter

1-2 cups College Inn culinary broth (white wine and herb)

Kosher salt and fresh-ground mill pepper

¾ cup all-purpose flour

2 cups fresh sliced mushrooms of choice (my choice is Portobello)

¼ cup good Italian Marsala wine

3 tablespoons fresh chopped Italian flat-leaf parsley

⅛ cup fresh grated Pecorino-Romano cheese

1 pound pancetta or good bacon, cubed

1 large sweet white onion, diced

2 long carrot sticks, cleaned and cubed

Directions:

On a large tray or foil, pour in the flour and grated cheese. Mix together well and dust each shank on both sides. Place them on a platter, then place in a large preheated Dutch oven, deep-sided skillet, or pan, with your evoo and ¼ stick of butter on high heat. Once melted, throw in your onions and carrots and cook down. Once translucent, place your dusted shanks in carefully with cooking tongs and lightly brown both sides. Remove, set on a warm platter, and cover with foil. In a large frying pan on high heat with 2 tablespoons of evoo, cook down your pancetta or bacon to a crispy texture but not burned. Now carefully (using long covered oven mitts), take your pancetta or bacon out and drain all the drippings and oil into your Dutch oven. Now pour your culinary broth into the Dutch oven on medium heat. Add the Marsala wine, the remaining butter, browned shanks, and pancetta/bacon bites and bring to a boil. Add salt and pepper to taste, then simmer with the lid on for 20 minutes. Add the lemon juice and the sliced mushrooms and cover for another 20 minutes. Check the shanks with a fork for tenderness. (You can also place the covered Dutch oven in a preheated oven at 400° for the last 20 minutes or so.) Then open the lid and stir. Sprinkle in the parsley. Cover and cook for 5 more minutes or so. Once done, remove lid and let simmer (no heat) for a few minutes, then plate and serve with the sauce you have created. It is really delicious with some good Italian bread for dipping!

BAKED ASPARAGUS

Ingredients:
3 pounds fresh asparagus
5 tablespoons Italian extra virgin olive oil (evoo)
Kosher salt and fresh-ground mill pepper
½ cup Italian breadcrumbs
¼ cup fresh grated Pecorino-Romano cheese

Directions:
In a large baking dish, take your asparagus and cut 2½ inches or more off the bottom stems. Spread 2½ tablespoons of evoo on the baking dish and lightly salt and pepper. Lay out your cut asparagus and cover with remaining evoo and salt and pepper again. Place the dish in a preheated oven at 375° for 3 minutes, then sprinkle the breadcrumbs over all of the asparagus and place back in the oven for 15 minutes or until they are tender. Sprinkle on the grated cheese and cook for another 5-6 minutes until cheese is melted. Remove and serve.

FRANK'S CREAMY MASHED POTATOES

Ingredients:

3 pounds potatoes, peeled and cubed in a deep pot filled with water to top of potatoes

1 cup half-and-half cream, milk, or heavy cream (the choice is up to you)

1 stick salted butter

Kosher salt and fresh-ground mill pepper

1 jar of your favorite beef gravy

Directions:

Take your pot of cubed potatoes, add ¼ cup salt, and place on high heat until boiling. Quickly bring down to a simmer with the lid on and cook for 25 minutes or until potatoes are fork tender. Once done, carefully drain out as much water as you can (I usually drain the pot in the inside part of the sink). Now add the whole stick of butter and, with an electric hand blender, start mashing your cooked potatoes along with the butter. Add ½ cup choice cream and keep blending and adding cream until the potatoes turn to soft, smooth, creamy texture. Once done, pour into a large serving bowl and enjoy. Use the heated beef gravy on top if you choose.

TORTA DI PATATE CON FORMAGGIO

(Potato Cheese Pie)

Ingredients:
3 pounds potatoes, peeled and cubed, in a deep pot with water to top of potatoes
1 stick salted butter
¼ cup seasoned Italian breadcrumbs
½ cup milk or half-and-half
6 oz prosciutto, sliced thin
6 oz sliced fresh mozzarella cheese
2 eggs
⅛ teaspoon fresh nutmeg
¾ cup fresh grated parmesan cheese
6 oz fresh sliced Provolone cheese
¼ cup fresh chopped Italian flat-leaf parsley
Kosher salt and fresh-ground mill pepper

Directions:
Take your pot of watered potatoes and add ¼ cup salt. Bring to a boil on high heat and then to a simmer for 25 minutes until potatoes are fork tender. Carefully drain out the water and place on the counter to cool. Now take a round baking dish and coat the inside with some butter all around. Sprinkle breadcrumbs inside and turn dish until the crumbs cover all. Preheat oven to 350°. Take the baking dish and pour in the cooked potatoes. Spread them all around and flatten as much as possible. In a large bowl, mix your eggs, cream of choice, and nutmeg with an electric blender on low. Add parmesan cheese, parsley, salt, and pepper, and blend until creamy. Once that is done, pour your mixture over the baking dish with the potatoes and place a layer of the prosciutto and a layer of mozzarella cheese evenly, along with a light dusting of breadcrumbs. Slice the re-maining butter and place on top all around. Finally spread a layer of the provolone cheese slices. Place in oven and bake for 35 minutes or until there is a golden crust on top. Once done, remove from the oven carefully, cool for 5 minutes, and serve.

SPADA CON ERBE

(Grilled Swordfish with Herbs)

Ingredients:

1 tablespoon fresh rosemary, minced
1 tablespoon fresh sage, chopped
1 teaspoon dried oregano
1 teaspoon fresh minced thyme (no stems)
6 tablespoons Italian extra virgin olive oil (evoo)
Kosher salt and fresh-ground mill pepper
2-3 tablespoons balsamic vinegar
3 tablespoons fresh-squeezed lemon juice
4 cloves fresh peeled garlic, chopped
4 fresh swordfish steaks, about 6-8 oz each

Directions:

The secret to this recipe is to marinate overnight. In a deep platter, place your swordfish steaks. In a large bowl, pour in all of your herbs. Add 4 tablespoons of evoo, balsamic vinegar, lemon juice, and the garlic. Mix together well and add salt and pepper to taste, then pour over your swordfish. Cover tightly with plastic wrap. Place in your refrigerator for 4 hours or longer (overnight is fine). Once ready to prepare, preheat your grill or grill pan on the stovetop. Brush grill surface with evoo. Place your swordfish steaks on grill surface and cook on both sides until golden brown, 2-3 minutes each side, not to overcook. Meanwhile in a sauté pan, pour in the marinade juice and bring to a light boil, then shut off. Once the swordfish steaks are done, plate and drizzle small amounts of the marinade over each steak and enjoy with a cold light Italian wine.

FILETTI DI SOGLIOLA ALLA MANDORLE

(Fillet of Sole with Almond Sauce)

Ingredients:
2 pounds fresh sole fillets
½ stick salted butter
8-10 sage leaves
¾ cup all-purpose flour
1½ tablespoons Italian flat-leaf parsley
¾ cup toasted almonds, chopped
Kosher salt and fresh-ground mill pepper
3-4 tablespoons Italian extra virgin olive oil (evoo)

Directions:
On a tray or sheet of foil, pour your flour and sprinkle with salt and pepper. Mix together with a fork, and dust each fillet in your mixture, shaking off any excess. Place in a large sauté pan that is on medium heat with 2 tablespoons of evoo and 3 pats of butter. Once melted, add your dusted fillets of sole and lightly brown both sides. Place them on a warm platter and cover. Quickly add evoo, remaining butter, and almonds, along with your herbs, salt, and pepper. Pour over your cooked fillets and serve.

SPAGHETTI ALLA PUTTANESCA

(Spaghetti from the Ladies of the Night)

Ingredients:
1 pound spaghetti or linguine
8 tablespoons Italian extra virgin olive oil (evoo)
1 can San Marzano plum tomatoes, chopped with juices
4 tablespoons drained capers
2 tablespoons oregano
3 teaspoons fresh minced Italian basil
4 oz oil-packed anchovies, chopped
¾ cup Calamata olives, drained and chopped
1 tablespoon red pepper flakes
6 cloves fresh minced garlic
1 teaspoon sugar
4 tablespoons Italian flat-leaf parsley, minced
Kosher salt and fresh-ground mill pepper

Directions:
In a large pot, add 4-6 quarts of water and bring to a boil. Add 4 tablespoons of salt to water. When boiling, add the pasta and cook for 8-10 minutes until al dente. In the meantime, in a large saucepan over medium heat, add 6 tablespoons of evoo and garlic. Cook to very a light color change, careful not to burn the garlic or you have to start over. Once cooked, add tomatoes, capers, olives, anchovies, red pepper flakes, basil, oregano, and finally sugar. Stir occasionally until thickened, about 15 minutes. Add salt and pepper to taste. Add the parsley mix and stir. Cook for 3 more minutes, then add your drained pasta and stir, and mix all. Add some pasta water if too dry (very little). Now pour into a serving bowl, sprinkle evoo on top, and serve.

CROSTONI E' MOZZARELLA

(Grilled Italian Toast with Mozzarella and Special Sauce)

Ingredients:
4-6 ripe tomatoes, cubed
12 oz fresh mozzarella, diced
1 small can Italian olive oil-packed anchovy fillets, minced, or a small jar of drained capers, minced (your choice or both)
8 tablespoons Italian extra virgin olive oil (evoo)
3 teaspoons oregano
Kosher salt and fresh-ground mill pepper
1 loaf good crusted Italian bread, sliced

Directions:
In a large bowl, place your cubed tomatoes. Salt and pepper lightly. Add the mozzarella, anchovies, oregano, 4 tablespoons of evoo, and salt and pepper to taste. Mix all together and let sit while you grill each slice of bread, with brushed evoo on both sides. Cook to a light brown on both sides and place on a large baking tray. Add your bowl mixture on each slice and place in a preheated oven at 375° for a few minutes until mozzarella starts to melt. Remove and serve. What a treat!

FRANK'S STRING BEAN SALAD
WITH RASPBERRY VINAIGRETTE SAUCE

Ingredients:

2 pounds fresh string beans, both ends cut off (just the tips) and boiled in water until tender

1 can red kidney beans or any bean of choice

2 pounds white potatoes, peeled, cubed, and boiled in water until fork tender and drained

6 tablespoons Italian extra virgin olive oil (evoo)

6-8 tablespoons Italian balsamic vinegar

6-8 tablespoons raspberry vinegar

1 small red onion, cleaned and diced

Kosher salt and fresh-ground mill pepper

2 tablespoons oregano

Directions:

In a large bowl, place your soft, cooked, cubed potatoes and string beans. Mix in a bowl with a large spoon, adding evoo and salt and pepper to taste. Add both vinegars to mix. Stir and taste. (You may need to add more ingredients.) Once done, add your oregano, mix, and leave to cool. Just serve and eat. What a treat!

BRODETTO ALLA MANIERA DI CATOLICA

(My Aunt's Recipe from Sicily)

Ingredients:

1 pound fresh cuttlefish, cleaned and cut in large cubes (can use any kind of meaty fish)

1 pound fresh red snapper fillets, cleaned and cubed

1 pound fresh sea bass, cleaned and cubed

1 pound fresh mullet, cleaned and cubed

1 pound fresh rockfish, cleaned and cubed

1 pound fresh cod, cleaned and cubed

1 pound fresh shrimp, shelled, cleaned, and veins removed

1 large sweet white onion, chopped

6 cloves fresh garlic, minced

1 large can San Marzano peeled tomatoes, hand crushed in a bowl

3 tablespoons chopped fresh Italian flat-leaf parsley

Sea salt and fresh-ground mill pepper

1½ cups Italian extra virgin olive oil (evoo)

4 cups good Italian light white wine

2 tablespoons sugar

1 teaspoon red pepper flakes

1 tablespoon oregano

1 tablespoon minced Italian flat-leaf parsley

3 cups College Inn culinary broth (white wine and herb)

Directions:

Heat a large Dutch oven pot on medium heat. Add 3 tablespoons of evoo, and add your onion. Sauté till translucent, and then add the garlic, cooking it to a very light color (do not burn. If so, start over). Add your crushed tomatoes in a bowl, and add salt and pepper moderately. Now add the sugar and red pepper flakes and bring to a low boil. Quickly add the wine and the broth. Now bring to another low boil. Add all of the fish but the shrimp (they cook very fast. If too long, they get tough), and bring to boil and then down to a simmer, adding the oregano and covering with the lid. Cook for about 25 minutes until fish is fork tender. Add the shrimp and parsley and cover for 5 minutes until shrimp is a pink color. Stir and let stand with the heat off for about 7 minutes. Uncover, serve in bowls with crusted Italian bread, and just enjoy. It's a little costly but good.

OYSTERS FRANKEFELLER (ROCKEFELLER) MY WAY

Ingredients:
1 stick salted butter
1 cup heavy cream
3 cloves fresh minced garlic
1 cup fresh grated Parmigianno-Reggieano cheese
¼ teaspoon fresh-ground nutmeg
½ teaspoon sea salt and fresh-ground mill pepper
2 cups baby spinach, chopped thin
½ cup good Italian pancetta or lean bacon
2 cups cooking rock salt on a large baking dish
¾ cup panko breadcrumbs
4 tablespoons Italian extra virgin olive oil (evoo)
2 dozen fresh oysters, cleaned, shucked, and still on a half shell, kept on ice to stay fresh
Sea salt and fresh-ground mill pepper

Directions:
Heat a sauté pan on medium heat. Add butter and garlic and cook to a light color (do not burn. If so start over) about 2 minutes. Add cream and turn heat to low while stirring and cream begins to steam (do not boil). Add the Parmigianno cheese, nutmeg, and light salt and pepper. Stir until cheese melts and when sauce is becoming thick. Add spinach, stir until it wilts into the sauce, then remove from heat. In another sauté pan with 2 tablespoons of evoo, melt down the pancetta/bacon until crispy. Preheat your oven to 500°. In your large baking dish with the cooking rock salt, lay out the iced oysters on the half shell on top of the cooking rock salt and spoon your spinach sauce over each oyster, along with some panko breadcrumbs, crispy pancetta/bacon, and Parmigianno-Reggieano cheese on top. Place the baking dish in the oven (make sure you wear long oven mitts) and cook for maybe 10 minutes or until golden light brown and bubbling. Remove, carefully plate each oyster with good tongs, and serve. To die for!

SEA BASS WITH CAPERS, OLIVES, AND TOMATOES

Note: In this recipe I'm using sea bass, but you may choose any other whitefish you like.

Ingredients:
2-4 oz fillets fresh cleaned sea bass
½ cup chopped calamata olives
4 tablespoons capers
1 medium-size sweet white onion, chopped
¼ teaspoon or less red pepper flakes
1 cup good Italian light white wine
2 cups Italian diced tomatoes and their juices
Kosher salt and fresh-ground mill pepper
3-4 cups fresh baby spinach leaves
5 tablespoons Italian extra virgin olive oil (evoo)
2 cloves minced garlic

Directions:
In a large, deep, nonstick sauté pan, add 3 tablespoons of evoo. On medium heat, carefully add your sea bass and lightly brown both sides until opaque in the center of the fish, basically 2-3 minutes per side or until they are fork tender. Then transfer to a warm platter and cover with foil to keep warm. In the same pan, add 2 more tablespoons of evoo, red pepper flakes, onion, and garlic, and sauté to light color (do not burn) for a few minutes. Add the wine, cook for 4 minutes, and add your diced tomatoes with the juices and 1 tablespoon of sugar. Cook to a low boil and add olives and capers. Bring down to a simmer. Stir in your spinach, cook for 3 minutes, season with salt and pepper to taste, and shut off. Take your platter of warm sea bass, pour on your sauce that you created, and serve.

SARDINE FRITTERS FROM SCIACCA

Ingredients:

1 can oil-packed sardines from Sicily, about two pounds chopped (not mashed) with their oils into small pieces (This is the only city in the world to get great sardines. They have been shipping them for centuries.).

1 cup Italian seasoned breadcrumbs

1 teaspoon fresh-ground mill pepper

½ teaspoon red pepper flakes

3 fresh eggs

3 tablespoons fresh milk

8 tablespoons Italian extra virgin olive oil (evoo)

¼ cup fresh grated parmesan cheese

6 tablespoons fresh chopped Italian flat-leaf parsley

Directions:

In a large bowl, add ½ cup breadcrumbs, pepper, parsley, red pepper flakes, and the sardines, also 2 tablespoons of grated cheese. Mix all together well (I recommend using your hands—after you wash them, of course). Now add 1 egg and mix, and start to roll your mixture into little small balls, maybe ping-pong size or smaller. In a bowl, add 2 eggs and milk and lightly mix with a large spoon. Once whipped, take each ball and roll it in the egg mix, coating it. In another bowl, add the rest of the breadcrumbs and roll the egg-washed balls in the crumbs, coating them completely. Take a large sauté pan/skillet and, on medium heat, add the evoo. Once ready, carefully add each ball in the pan and lightly brown each sardine ball all around, using tongs, careful not to squeeze too hard and break them. Once browned in the pan, take them out and lay them on a tray with paper towels to drain the excess oil. Sprinkle them with grated cheese, plate, and serve.

SEARED SEA SCALLOPS
IN LEMON BUTTER CAPER SAUCE

Ingredients:
1½ pounds fresh cleaned sea scallops
½ stick salted butter
½ cup fresh-squeezed lemon juice
½ cup good Italian light white wine
¼-½ cups heavy cream
4 cloves fresh thin-sliced garlic
6 tablespoons Italian extra virgin olive oil (evoo)
1 jar drained capers
2 tablespoons fresh chopped Italian flat-leaf parsley
Kosher salt and fresh-ground mill pepper

Directions:
In a large bowl, place the sea scallops and season with salt and pepper, lightly coating them. In a large, deep-side, nonstick sauté pan, add the evoo, butter, and garlic. On medium heat, lightly cook the garlic (do not burn. If so start over). Now add in the sea scallops and sear on all sides. Once seared, remove and place on a tray with paper towels to drain. Now quickly add the wine and heavy cream into pan and stir with a wooden spoon for 2 minutes to low boil. Simmer, stir again, and add all of your sea scallops. Roll in sauce for 2 minutes, coating them. Then on a serving platter, place your cooked sea scallops, pour your sauce over them, serve, and enjoy.

FRANK'S FAMOUS STUFFED MUSHROOM CAPS

Ingredients:

12-20 large mushroom caps, brushed clean (never wash the mushroom, always brush gently clean), stems removed and placed to the side

¾ cup toasted and chopped pine nuts, (in a small pan, just lightly toast them; do not burn and lightly chop)

8 green onion stalks, peeled and chopped into small little rings

1½ pounds Prosiutto/good bacon, chopped

1½ 8-oz tubs Mascarpone Italian sweet cream cheese

1 cup panko breadcrumbs

5 cloves fresh minced garlic

¾ cup Italian Marsala wine

½ cup Italian extra virgin olive oil (evoo)

¼ cup finally chopped Italian flat-leaf parsley (just the leaves, no stems)

½ stick salted butter

Directions:

In an extra-large bowl, place each cap upside down. Try not stack them on each other. Sprinkle them with evoo and Marsala wine and let soak for a half-hour. In the meantime, take the mushroom stems and slice off the bottom hard ends, about 1/8 inch. Chop them into small pieces (the smaller, the better). In a large nonstick pan on medium heat, add evoo, butter, and the prosciutto/bacon, and cook down but not too crispy. Then add garlic, green onion rings, chopped stems, chopped pine nuts, and panko crumbs. Stir and cook on low heat for about 10-15 minutes, but always keep stirring the ingredients so nothing burns. As this is cooking, lay out your soaked mushroom caps on a large baking tray with nonstick foil with the bottoms up and drain all leftover evoo and Marsala into each cap. Once your mixture is at a low bubble, turn off heat, add in the Mascarpone cream cheese, and gently mix until it is all melted together. Let cool for 3 minutes and carefully, with a teaspoon, stuff each mushroom cap with your creation. Once all are filled, any extra filling just pile onto each cap and place tray into a 350° preheated oven. Bake for 15-20 minutes or when the juices start flowing out of the cap. Remove, gently plate them on a serving platter, and spoon any mixture left onto baking the tray. Now it's time to enjoy your creation. They also can be refrigerated. If there are any leftovers, microwave to eat again.

FRANK'S PESE AL LEMONE A FORNO

(Oven-Baked Fish in Lemon)

Note: Please be advised that you can use any type of whole fish or fillets of your choice. For any whole fish you buy, have a professional fish monger clean and descale.

Ingredients:
1 whole cleaned red snapper or fillets (your choice), 3-4-pounds
1 20-inch sheet heavy-duty aluminum foil
⅓ cup Italian extra virgin olive oil (evoo)
Kosher salt and fresh-ground mill pepper
2 whole lemons, sliced thin
5 tablespoons drained capers
4 whole sprigs fresh Italian flat-leaf parsley

Directions:
Take your whole fish, rinse under cold water, and dry with paper towels. If needed, cut off all fins.

Now with a sharp knife, sore both sides of the fish skins with an across pattern. Do not go too deep into the flesh. Take the foil, lay flat on your working area, and spread a little evoo, salt, and pepper in the area where you are laying the fish. Now open the center cavity of the fish, salt and pepper well, pour some evoo, and start stuffing lemon slices and some capers in the cavity. Now brush evoo all over the top and sides, and salt and pepper well. Fill the whole top of the fish from head to tail with lemon slices and capers. Now lay as many parsley sprigs as you can on the fish and in the cavity if possible. (Optional: Some of my friends love when I pour some soy sauce on top.) Take the long sides of the foil and bring together. Fold together the top part like you're making a tent. Fold the outer sides together, and you should have a tent look. This makes the fish cook in a steam bath. Now place on a tray and put in a 375° preheated oven for 60 minutes depending on size. Once done, place on a large serving tray and, gently and carefully, open tops and sides. Now it's time to enjoy your creation. The skin should just peel off with the edge of a knife, and meat will be soft. After you remove the top layer of meat, be careful of those tiny bones. With a knife, just lift the tail, and bottom layers of meat should stay on the foil. Pull the tail, and the skeleton and head will pull out. Discard and enjoy the bottom layer. Some pick on the head. It is truly a great dish.

PESE MARINARA AL FORNO

(Baked Whole Fish in Tomato Sauce)

Ingredients:
1 whole cleaned red snapper, 3-4 pounds
Heavy-duty aluminum foil
⅓ cup Italian extra virgin olive oil (evoo)
Kosher salt and fresh-ground mill pepper
1 large can San Marzano plum tomatoes
5 tablespoons drained capers
1 tablespoon sugar
6 cloves fresh thin-sliced garlic
6 sprigs Italian flat-leaf parsley

Directions:
Take your whole snapper, rinse under cold water, and pat dry with paper towels. Now with a sharp knife, score both sides of the fish in a cross pattern, not too deep, into the meat of the fish. Cut off all of its fins. Lay the foil flat on your work area and spread some evoo, salt, and pepper in the center, where the fish will lie. Take your fish and add evoo and salt and pepper to the center cavity well. Lay it on its side and brush evoo all over on top and sides. Now lift all of the sides of the foil, create a well, and gently hand crush the plum tomatoes over the fish, not splashing the juices all over the place, just on the fish. Stuff some of the tomatoes and also the capers inside the cavity. Cover top of fish with remaining tomatoes and capers, sprinkle sugar over top, and lay all of the parsley sprigs all around inside the cavity and on top. Close the foil, creating a tent-like finish tightly all around. You want to create a cone so the fish cooks in a steam bath. On a large baking tray, lay your foiled fish and place in a 375° preheated oven for 60 minutes. When done, open the top of the foil, and the skin should just peel off. If not, cook for another 10-15 minutes (this all depends on size and oven make). Once done, remove, place foiled fish on a serving platter, and carefully open all sides, leaving fish and juices in a well. Peel off skin or eat as is. Enjoy top layer/fillet, then with a knife just insert between the tail and the bottom fillet of the meat. Lift the tail gently, and you should be able to lift the whole skeleton and head off and discard them or, like some, pick on the head. Watch out for the tiny bones. Enjoy a very tasty dish.

POLLO E' SALSICCIA
CON E' PEPERONI ARROSTITI AL FORNO

Ingredients:

5 pounds fresh trimmed chicken parts (legs, thighs, wings, breasts)

6 links Italian sausages, sweet or hot or both

2 large thinly sliced sweet white onions

6 large peppers (2 red, 2 orange, 2 yellow), all sliced into strips, no seeds

10 cloves fresh thin-sliced garlic, not chopped

2 cups Italian extra virgin olive oil (evoo)

8 sprigs rosemary

8 sprigs sage

8 sprigs thyme

1 bottle Italian light white wine

6 large Yukon gold potatoes, peeled and cubed

10-12 sprigs Italian flat-leaf parsley

Sea salt and fresh-ground mill pepper

1 stick salted butter

Directions:

In an extra-large bowl, place the chicken, sausage, ½ cup of evoo, 3 tablespoons of salt, and 3 tablespoons of ground pepper, and hand mix well and then coat. (If you do not have a large-enough bowl, do them separately.) In a large Dutch oven, add ½ stick of butter and 1 cup of evoo on medium heat. When it is hot and the butter is disappearing, add very carefully, using cooking tongs, the chicken and sausage, lightly browning all sides (do not burn; keep turning your meats). Once all is browned, place on a tray with paper towels to absorb any extra oil. Drain your pan and add ½ cup evoo and ½ stick of butter, still on medium heat, and then add onions and potatoes. Sauté for 8 minutes while stirring. Now add 1 cup of white wine, your garlic, peppers, and the herbs—except the parsley—and cook for 10 minutes while stirring occasionally. Now place all of the chicken and sausage, the remaining evoo and wine, and salt and pepper freely. Preheat your oven to 450°, and now give everything a good stir. Place the lid on and put in the oven for 15 minutes, then lower the temperature to 325° and cook for 20 minutes or until fork tender. If it looks a little dry while cooking, add water, ½ cup at a time, not too much. Once it's done, remove and open the lid. Sprinkle with the parsley, and add salt and pepper to taste. Close lid, let stand for 5 minutes, open, and serve.

FRANK'S CARNE AL FORNO

(Oven-Cooked Meat)

Ingredients:

½ pound 1-oz cubed veal, chicken breast, pork, duck breast, and lamb (no bones), totaling 2½ lbs

2 fresh carrot stalks, cleaned and chopped

2 medium-size sweet white onions, chopped

4 cloves fresh garlic, chopped

3 fresh celery stalks, cleaned and chopped

¼ cup Italian extra virgin olive oil (evoo)

Sea salt and fresh-ground mill pepper

2 cups College Inn culinary broth (white wine and herb)

3 cups good Italian red wine

2 tablespoons fresh chopped Italian flat-leaf parsley

1 tablespoon fresh chopped Italian basil

1 large can San Marzano plum tomatoes, hand crushed in a bowl

2 tablespoons sugar

Directions:

In a large Dutch oven, add ⅛ cup of evoo on medium-high heat. After 2 minutes, start to gently lightly brown your meats on all sides. When done, put meats in a bowl and cover with foil. Now add remaining evoo in same Dutch oven and start to sauté your onions, carrots, celery, and garlic for 5 minutes, then add 2 tablespoons of salt and 2 tablespoons of ground pepper. In 2 minutes, add your wine, broth, tomatoes with juice, and 2 table-spoon of sugar. Stir for 1 minute, then add all of your meats, bring to a boil, and simmer for 10 minutes. Stir well and cover with the lid for 2 more minutes. Preheat your oven to 350° and cook for a good 15-20 minutes until fork tender. Stir every once in a while. Add only little water if needed. When done, remove, add salt and pepper to taste, add herbs, and stir. Cover with lid and leave standing for 5-7 minutes, and then start serving. You'll really enjoy this dish. You can serve over rice or pasta of choice, and yes, do not forget to dunk crusty Italian bread!

Note: This dish can also be cooked on a stovetop on a slow simmer for 3 ½ hours with the lid on. Also, it can be cooked in a slow cooker all day.

FRANK'S WAY OF MAKING LEG OF BABY LAMB

Ingredients:

3 pounds leg of baby lamb (ask your butcher to debone and tie)

2 cups good Italian red wine

¼ cup Italian extra virgin olive oil (evoo)

10 cloves fresh sliced garlic

6 sprigs fresh rosemary, chopped

6 sprigs fresh sage, chopped

¼ cup sugar (cane or brown, your choice)

1½ cups College Inn culinary broth (white wine and herb)

Kosher salt and fresh-ground mill pepper

1 extra-large freezer bag

⅓ cup all-purpose flour

¼ cup fresh chopped Italian flat-leaf parsley

1 large sweet white onion, thinly sliced

Directions:

Unroll your leg of lamb, lay flat, and give a good sprinkle of salt and ground pepper, then take half of your garlic and spread all over, along with half of the rosemary and sage. Then sprinkle some evoo over all. Now carefully on one end, start rolling the lamb until it is round again and you did not lose any of the ingredients. Retie with butcher's twine across the whole leg, about 4-6 bands 2 inches apart. On a tray or work area, brush the whole leg with evoo, salt, and pepper. Now with a sharp pointed knife, make about 8 1-½-inch slits into the meat, fat side up. Stuff each slit with garlic, rosemary, and sage using your finger to insert the ingredients. Now take the freezer bag and place your meats inside. Pour in 8 tablespoons of salt and 5 tablespoons of fresh-ground pepper, red wine, and broth, along with the sugar and onions. Now seal the bag and shake the bag carefully to mix all ingredients. On a platter, place in the refrigerator for 16-24 hours. After refrigeration, place on counter and let set for 30-40 minutes in the bag. Now carefully open and remove the lamb, careful not to lose any of the juices, and seal closed again, holding in all of the marinade. Take the lamb and dry with paper towels. On a sheet of foil, pour your flour, roll the lamb all around, and coat well. In a large Dutch oven, add remaining evoo (about 3 tablespoons) and place on high heat. When ready, gently place lamb in and lightly brown all sides. While it is browning, preheat your oven to 375°. Now when finished browning the lamb, carefully pour the bag of marinade completely over your lamb and bring to a boil. Now quickly shut off heat, place lid on top, and place in your preheated oven for 40-50 minutes, then check and if needed pour ½ to 1 cup of red wine. Cover and cook for another10 minutes and insert a thermometer to check for a 125° to130° temperature for rare, 135° to 140° for medium to well. Remove and place on cutting platter. Sprinkle with the parsley. Then just slice and serve, and be careful of the twine (remove first). This is a classic dish.

MY INSALATA DI POMODORE E' CIPOLLE

(My Tomato and Onion Salad)

Ingredients:
10-12 ripe red juice tomatoes, sliced into small wedges
1 cup Italian extra virgin olive oil (evoo)
1½ large sweet white onions, thinly sliced
1½ teaspoons dried oregano
2 cucumbers, peeled and sliced
1 cup leaves of basil
Kosher salt and fresh-ground mill pepper
Bottle of good Italian red wine vinegar

Directions:
In a large bowl, place your tomato wedges, along with the onions and cucumbers. With a large wooden knife and spoon, give a gentle toss to mix all. Then pour over evoo, sprinkle salt and pepper, toss, and mix well. Pour ½ cup of vinegar, now add the oregano and hand rip each basil leaf into small pieces. Toss and toss over again and taste for salt and pepper, adding more if needed. You can start to eat your salad now or cover the top with clear wrap and refrigerate for a few hours or overnight. Then place on the counter for a half-hour, remove wrap, give it a good mix, and start to enjoy. Overnight all of the favors came together, and with good crusty Italian bread, believe me, there is none better!

ZUPPA DI VONGOLE SICILIANO

(Cooked Clams Sicilian Style)

Ingredients:

25-30 fresh littleneck or small cherrystone clams

4 tablespoons oatmeal

2 bottles clam juice

2 cups good Italian light white wine

1½ teaspoons oregano, fresh or dry

1½ tablespoons fresh minced Italian flat-leaf parsley

1 or 1½ teaspoons red pepper flakes (your choice)

7 cloves fresh thin-sliced garlic

2½ tablespoons fresh chopped basil

1 to 2 cans San Marzano Italian plum tomatoes, hand crushed in a bowl with 2 tablespoons sugar mixed in by hand

½ cup Italian extra virgin olive oil (evoo)

Sea salt and fresh-ground mill pepper

Directions:

To clean the clams, rinse under cold water with a brittle brush, cleaning off any deposits on shells. Discard any clams that are open. Place remaining clams in a deep bowl with ice and water to top of the clams, along with 4 tablespoons of oatmeal and 4 tablespoons of salt, which draws out any sand in the clams, for a half-hour or longer, as long as you add ice to keep cold. Take your bowl of iced clams and rinse under cold running water, removing all oatmeal and any sand. Place in a large colander and let stand in the sink to drain. In a large deep-sided saucepan on medium to high heat, add evoo and garlic and lightly sauté for 2 minutes (do not burn or start over).

Now add your clams and, with a large wooden spoon, gently toss all around for a minute. Add your wine and bowl of tomatoes, red pepper flakes, oregano, and basil, and stir well. Add salt and pepper to taste and bring to a boil. Then cover with a lid and bring down to a simmer. Cook for 10-15 minutes or until all of the clams are wide open. When done, first discard any clams that are still closed, and now pour your creation into a large serving bowl. Serve by scooping into each bowl, then dip with good Italian bread and eat the clams. OMG! What a dish!

FRANK'S CLAM CHOWDER

Ingredients:
6-8 Yukon potatoes, peeled and diced into small cubes and sitting in water
3 stalks celery, cleaned and chopped
1½ large sweet white onions, chopped
3 cups baby clams, littleneck clams, and oysters, chopped with their juices in a bowl, fresh, without the shells
Sea salt and fresh-ground mill pepper
4 tablespoons Italian extra virgin olive oil (evoo)
½ pound salt pork, diced
1 cup all-purpose flour
1 stick salted butter
2 pints half-and-half cream
2 pints heavy cream
1 pound diced pancetta or bacon
Worcestershire sauce
2 bottles clam juice
2 cups spring water

Directions:
Note: Step 1 and step 2 must be started at the same time.

Step 1: In a sauté pan with a lid on medium heat, add 2 tablespoons of evoo, add the bacon and salt pork, and reduce to a soft texture, not crispy. Add the onions and butter. Once melted, stir in the flour on low heat and add 1 pint of half-and-half at a time. Add salt and pepper and continuously stir, adding 2 tablespoons of Worcestershire sauce and stirring until it turns a soft rue.

Step 2: In a large Dutch oven pot, add 2 cups of spring water, clam juice, and potatoes, and bring to a boil. When potatoes are fork tender, reduce to half heat. Add clams and oysters and juices, and lightly salt and pepper (a little heavy on the ground mill pepper). Stir and cook for 5 minutes, and now you take Step 1 and pour into Step 2. Add the heavy cream and stir. Cover with a lid and simmer for 30 minutes, checking the consistency. If it is too chunky, you can use a hand-power chopper to make it smooth. Once you have acceptable texture and taste (add salt and pepper if needed), then just start to serve into bowls for everyone to eat.

Also, please note that I have made this and have added frozen sweet corn and 2 tablespoons of cornstarch for thickness. It's all up to you. Don't forget, you do not have to be afraid to experiment. When everything is fresh, how bad can it be? Enjoy!

TUTTA A' FRITTATA

———◦———

(Everything in an Omelet Creation)

In Italy and at my house, no leftover food is thrown away. It's turned into a frittata (omelet). Eggs can glue anything together and combine all foods. Please understand that omelets are endless in what you can add: leftover meats, vegetables, broccoli, garlic, chicken livers, onions, cheeses, spinach, olives, peppers, potatoes, sardines, capers, sausage, cooked fish, tomatoes—the list goes on. So many choices. It's up to you!

Ingredients:
6 eggs (or more, depending on your creation)
Italian extra virgin olive oil (evoo)
½ stick salted butter
1-½ cups fresh grated cheese of choice
Kosher salt and fresh-ground mill pepper

Directions:
Take any leftover items of choice that are also fresh and chop them up with a sharp knife. In a large nonstick pan on medium heat, add evoo as needed. You'll be the judge. Add butter, your other ingredients, and stir. Add salt and pepper to taste. In the meantime, in a bowl crack your eggs and add some half-and-half, milk, or heavy cream, and whisk to a creamy texture, adding a little salt and pepper and grated cheese. Once your leftovers are steaming, add your egg mix and pour into a pan. Gently spread the egg mix all around and into the leftovers. Put on simmer and wait for the egg mix to harden and brown. Slide out of the pan onto a platter, cut, and serve. It's just that easy. Remember, you can create anything you want!

MY GRILLED STEAK
WITH OYSTER MUSHROOM SAUCE

Ingredients:

2-3 pounds porterhouse steak, trimmed

1 cup fresh oysters in their juices

3 cups sliced oyster mushrooms

1 cup heavy cream

½ stick salted butter

1 minced fresh shallot

3 cloves fresh thin-sliced garlic

Kosher salt and fresh-ground mill pepper

1 tablespoon Worcestershire sauce

3 tablespoons Italian Extra virgin olive oil (evoo)

2 cups veal stock (College Inn culinary broth)

Directions:

In a nonstick sauté pan on medium heat, add ½ of the butter and melt. Add shallot and garlic for 2 minutes, then add 2 cups of stock and cream and stir. Cook for 4-5 minutes on simmer. Add the cup of oysters. Stir for a minute, and add a pinch of salt and some ground pepper. Add 1 tablespoon of Worcestershire sauce, stir, and cook for 10-12 minutes until reduced. While this is cooking, in another nonstick pan add 3 tablespoons of evoo and remaining butter. Melt down and add the mushrooms. Stir and cover with lid for 5-7 minutes until wilted, then pour them into your other pan and stir.

Now on a grill pan or outside grill on high heat, quickly brush evoo over grills or pan. Once smoky, layer your steak on the grill or pan, close cover or place pot lid on top of a grill pan to create a dome, and cook for 4½minutes on each side for rare and longer for well done. Once cooked, place on a large platter a layer of your oyster mushroom sauce first, then place your steak and remaining sauce on top.

This a rich dish, but it's to die for. Wait until you taste it! You be the judge. Enjoy!

ARAGOSTA OREGANATA

(Baked Lobster)

Ingredients:
2 2-pound lobsters, fresh and alive
8 tablespoons Italian extra virgin olive oil (evoo)
2 teaspoons fresh chopped sweet basil
4 cloves fresh minced garlic
2 tablespoons fresh chopped Italian flat-leaf parsley
½ cup fresh grated parmesan cheese
1 cup Italian seasoned breadcrumbs
1 teaspoon fresh or dry oregano
1 cup College Inn culinary broth (white wine and herb)

Directions:
After making sure their claws are tied, place your live lobsters in the freezer for 30 minutes. This will make them dormant. Then remove and insert a sharp butcher knife down the middle and split them into two sides, shell sides down. Now remove a small sac just in back of the head of the lobster and discard. Place them on a large baking tray with nonstick foil under them, cut sides up. Now take the claws and gently crack them, removing any broken shells, and lay them on the baking tray with the others.

In a bowl, mix in breadcrumbs, parsley, basil, cheese, oregano, garlic, ¼ cup evoo, broth, salt, and pepper. Lightly mix with a large spoon or by hand and make into a paste consistency. Now take your mixture and stuff it into the lobster parts, packing it in tightly. Place them in the oven on low broil and let cook 15 minutes or until the lobster shells are bright red and the meat is fork tender. Serve hot and enjoy.

LOBSTER AL MARE

(Zia Nina's Lobster Recipe from Sicily)

Ingredients:
2 2-pound lobsters, fresh and alive
1 gallon of seawater (if you don't live by the sea, mix heavy sea salt (¼ lb) into1 gallon of water for 2 days, shaking it every couple of hours)
1 pound seaweed
2 sticks of butter

Directions:
In an extra-large pot, add the seawater and seaweed until boiling, then add in your live lobster (I know it's painful to watch, but it's great to eat). Cook for about 12-15 minutes. Meanwhile, melt your butter in different little bowls (cover each bowl with clear wrap and microwave for 45 seconds). Now if the lobsters are done, plate and dip with hot melted butter. Just finger-licking good!

ARAGOSTA FRA DI' AVOLA

(My Aunt's Recipe for Lobster Cooked by the Devil)

Ingredients:
2 2-pound lobsters, fresh and alive
4 cloves fresh chopped garlic
¼ cup Italian extra virgin olive oil (evoo)
½ to 1 teaspoons red pepper flakes (it is up to you)
1 can San Marzano plum tomatoes, hand crushed in a bowl with juices
2 tablespoons fresh chopped Italian flat-leaf parsley
1 teaspoon oregano
Sea salt and fresh-ground mill pepper
2 tablespoons sugar

Directions:
Place your claw-tied live lobsters in the freezer for 30 minutes, which will make them dormant. Then remove and insert a sharp butcher knife straight down the middle and split into two sides. Remove the sac from behind the head of the lobster and discard. Take claws and gently crack them, removing the shells and the tail. Give all of the lobster meat a good chop with your butcher knife, and also keep the head and little claws together. They'll give your sauce a great favor. Now start on your sauce.

In a large, deep, nonstick pan, pour remaining evoo on medium heat and lightly brown garlic (do not burn. If so start over) for about 2 minutes. Now add your hand-crushed tomatoes and juices with 2 tablespoons of sugar and stir, adding the parsley, red pepper flakes, and oregano. Stir, turn down to simmer, and heat for 15 minutes. Place all of your lobster parts in a large, deep baking dish and pour in your sauce carefully so as not to burn yourself. Give it a good stir, and place the dish in a 350° preheated oven for 25-30 minutes or until lobster meat is fork tender. Now you can serve over cooked rice or pasta or just with good plain Italian crusty bread, your choice.

LOBSTER FRA DI' AVOLA ALLA FRANK

Ingredients:

2 2-pound lobsters, fresh and alive

1 large sweet white onion, chopped

1 24-oz can San Marzano plum tomatoes, hand crushed in a bowl with the juices

2 tablespoons sugar

½ cup Italian extra virgin olive oil (evoo)

½ to 1 teaspoon red pepper flakes (your choice)

3 cloves fresh thin-sliced garlic

1 teaspoon oregano

2 tablespoons chopped fresh Italian flat-leaf parsley

Sea salt and fresh-ground mill pepper

1 pound thin spaghetti

1 cup good Italian red wine

Directions:

Place your live lobsters in the freezer for 30 minutes. This will make them dormant. Now in a large deep-sided saucepan on medium heat, pour about 4 tablespoons of evoo and add the onions. Add salt and pepper and red pepper flakes, along with 2 more tablespoons of evoo. Once onions are translucent, add in your garlic and cook for 2 minutes, stirring occasionally. Now add your wine, crushed tomatoes with juices, parsley, oregano, sugar, and salt and pepper to taste. Bring to a low boil and simmer for at least 45 minutes with the lid on, stirring every 10 minutes.

Take your lobsters out and, with a sharp butcher knife, cut between the tail and head and separate. In the back of the head, there is a sac that you need to remove and discard. Chop remaining small claws, legs, and head with a knife and remove any loose shells. Crack the claws and split the tail in two. Take all of your lobster parts, add them to your sauce and stir well, coating all. Recover and cook until the lobster shell is bright red, roughly 12 minutes or so. When your pasta water has begun boiling, add 4 tablespoons of salt and cook your pasta as directed on the package. Drain well and pour into a large serving bowl. Pour in your lobster and the sauce, and toss gently, coating the pasta with the lobster flavor. Now just serve. What a treat!

STANDING RIB ROAST
WITH MUSTARD HERB CRUST

Ingredients:

5-6 pounds standing rib roast (Have your butcher debone and tie with the bones. That way the ribs are used as a rack for cooking.)

Kosher salt and fresh-ground mill pepper

3 tablespoons fresh chopped Italian flat-leaf parsley

3 tablespoons fresh chopped rosemary

¼ cup good Dijon mustard

¼ cup Italian extra virgin olive oil (evoo)

2 cups good Italian red wine

Directions:

In a large roasting pan, place the roast and get it to room temperature (if right out of the refrigerator). Then brush evoo all around the roast, coating it completely. Then heavily salt and pepper all sides. In a small bowl, add mustard, herbs, and remaining evoo. With brush, mix all together, add salt and pepper accordingly, and mix. Now brush your mixture all around roast in the pan with the ribs on the bottom as a rack (just the way the butcher tied for you) and pour in the wine. Place in a 400° preheated oven for 1 hour. Now remove, set on heat-padded surface, carefully reapply mixture again, coating roast, and set back in oven. Reset temperature to 325° and roast for 1 to 1½ hours more. Using a good meat thermometer, stick into center of roast and check temperature, 130° for rare, 140° for medium, and 145° to150° for well done. It is your choice (mine is rare, if you want to know). Once desired temperature is reached, remove from oven, place on safe surface, and cover with foil for 15 minutes. This lets all of the juices flow back into the meat. Now it's time to serve carefully. Cut off all of the twine, slice with a sharp knife to your desired size, and plate. Sprinkle some of the juice from the pan. This is really one of my favorite meats. Trust me, you'll love it!

FETTUCCINE AL' FREDO

Ingredients:
1 pound fresh fettuccine pasta
½ stick salted butter
1 cup heavy cream
1 cup fresh grated parmesan cheese
5-6 sage leaves
1 teaspoon fresh-ground nutmeg
Kosher salt and ground mill pepper

Direction:
Boil 3-4-quarts of water with lid on top. Add 4 tablespoons of salt. In a large, deep sauté pan on medium heat, add butter. As it melts, add the sage leaves and lightly salt and pepper. Stir butter and sage on low heat. Then add cream and ½ cup of grated cheese, and stir. Now drop your fresh pasta into the boiling water and cook for 3-4 minutes (fresh pasta cooks quickly). Gently drain the pasta and add it quickly into the saucepan, gently tossing it around, coating the pasta. Shut off the heat and sprinkle the nutmeg and remaining grated cheese on top. With tongs, grab some pasta and, in a twisting direction, place on serving plates. Spoon extra sauce on top. This is a delicious dish. Enjoy!

FRANK'S SICILIAN-STYLE
MACARONI AND CHEESE

Ingredients:
1 pound elbow pasta
1½ cups fresh shredded mozzarella cheese
1½ cups fresh shredded cheddar cheese
¾ cup fresh grated parmesan cheese
4 cups milk or half-and-half
⅓ cup toasted and chopped pine nuts
½ pound minced pancetta (Italian bacon)
Kosher salt and fresh-ground mill pepper
½ stick salted butter
1½ cups Italian seasoned breadcrumbs, toasted

Directions:
Start boiling 3-4 quarts of water. Once boiling, add 4 tablespoons of salt.

In a large nonstick sauté pan on medium heat, add 2 tablespoons of butter. Add pancetta (not too crispy), cook, then on low heat, add milk and cheese and start to melt together. Lightly salt and pepper and whisk gently as it thickens. In another nonstick pan on medium heat, add the butter melt, pour in breadcrumbs and pine nuts, and lightly toast for 2 minutes.

Now add pasta to the boiling water and cook for 2 minutes less than the instructions say. Once cooked, drain pasta, add into your sauce mixture, blend all together, carefully pour in a large deep-sided baking dish, and pour in your toasted crumbs and nuts, covering the whole top of the baking dish. Place in a preheated 425° oven for 20-25 minutes until the top is brown and bubbling. Remove from the oven and let cool for 3 minutes. Scoop and serve.

PASTA CON PESTO

Ingredients:
10 cloves fresh peeled garlic
3 cups fresh Italian basil leaves
1½ cups pistachio nuts (understand that in making pesto, you can use any type of nut that you like.)
1 to 1½ cups Italian extra virgin olive oil (evoo)
3 tablespoons sea salt
½ cup your favorite fresh grated cheese
1 pound your favorite pasta
Fresh-ground mill pepper

Directions:
Take your food processor and pour in the garlic, basil, nuts, and salt with 2 tablespoons of fresh-ground mill pepper. Start to blend on low pulses. When you reach a minced look, start to pour in the evoo until it becomes a creamy mixture. Then stop with evoo. Open and scoop all out into a container or bowl. You have now created pesto.

Boil 3-4 quarts of water. Then add 4 tablespoons of salt. Add the pasta, cooked as instructed on the package. Drain and pour on serving bowl, topped with your pesto. Mix and serve. Pesto needs not to be heated. Add hot drained pasta and toss for a tasty treat. Well, enjoy!

LUCINDA'S ORZO SALAD

(My Wife's Recipe)

Ingredients:
1 16-oz package of orzo pasta
8-10 cups College Inn culinary broth (white wine and herbs)
1 large bag frozen broccoli (you may choose any frozen veggie)
1 large red onion, peeled and chopped into small pieces
1 package cherry or grape tomatoes, sliced in half
2 cans washed and drained canned beans or your own, soaked in water overnight, boiled for a few hours, and cooled down
½ cup fresh chopped Italian flat-leaf parsley
½ cup fresh chopped Italian sweet basil
½ cup Italian extra virgin olive oil (evoo)
½ cup good Italian red wine vinegar
2 cups fresh-squeezed lemon juice
6 cloves fresh minced garlic
8 pieces sundried tomatoes, packaged in oil and chopped into small pieces
5 stalks celery, leaks, or green onions, cleaned, washed, and chopped into small pieces
Kosher salt and fresh-ground mill pepper
1 cup calamata olives, chopped
¾ cup chopped pine nuts, toasted
1 small jar Italian imported capers, drained

Directions: In a pasta pot, add the broth and bring to a boil. Then add the orzo pasta and the frozen veggies. Cover and cook for 10 minutes. Then remove, drain, pour into an extra-large serving bowl, and let cool. In the meantime, in a large bowl add all cherry or grape tomatoes, onion, beans, parsley, basil, sundried tomatoes, celery (or other choice), olives, and pine nuts. With a large wooden spoon, gently toss together all ingredients. Now add the evoo, lemon juice, vinegar, and garlic, and mix all together with a spoon. After 15 minutes of stirring occasionally, pour the mixture into your serving bowl with orzo and veggies, and again mix all together. Add salt and pepper to taste, and if needed add extra evoo and lemon juice and mix. Finally, cover top with clear wrap and store in refrigerator overnight. On occasion, give it a good stir, then remove. Place on counter and get to room temperature, stir, and serve.

FRANK'S FAMOUS LEMON CHICKEN
WITH FLAVORED RICE

Ingredients:

20 pieces chicken thighs and legs, trimmed of all fat and skin

3 cups fresh-squeezed lemon juice

1/4 cup good Italian red wine vinegar

6 cloves fresh peeled and chopped garlic

1½ cups Italian extra virgin olive oil (evoo)

1 tablespoon oregano

Kosher salt and fresh-ground mill pepper

2 containers 32-oz College Inn culinary broth (white wine and herbs)

3 cups long-grain rice

1 stick salted butter

Directions:

In a large pot, add the broth and bring to a boil. Add the butter, and once melted add rice and stir for 10 seconds. Place on simmer with the lid and cook for 20 minutes, then stir and shut off heat. Keep covered on the stove for 7 minutes. Check. Stir and serve when chicken is ready.

Line a large baking tray with nonstick foil. Brush with evoo and add a light coat of salt and pepper. Now lay out chicken pieces, bone up, and sprinkle with evoo, salt, and pepper. Place in a preheated oven at 375° for 22 minutes, then turn over all chicken and cook for another 20 minutes or until meat is browned and fork tender (not burned).

Meanwhile, in a large bowl add the cup of evoo, garlic, lemon juice, red wine vinegar, oregano, 1½ tablespoons of salt, and 2 tablespoons of fresh-ground mill pepper. Whisk to combine all of the flavors. Cover with clear wrap and place in the refrigerator until chicken is done. Then remove and microwave for 1 minute. Now, using a pair of tongs, take the cooked chicken parts and place them in an extra-large bowl. Pour your sauce over all and enjoy!

MY ITALIAN SAUSAGES
WITH PEPPERS AND ONIONS

Ingredients:
4 large green peppers
4 large red peppers
4 large yellow peppers
4 large orange peppers
(Note: Thinly slice all of the peppers and remove all seeds)
½ cup Italian extra virgin olive oil (evoo)
Kosher salt and fresh-ground mill pepper
8 links sweet or hot Italian sausages or a mixture of both
3 large sweet white onions, peeled and thinly sliced

Directions:
On a large baking tray lined with heavy-duty foil (for easy cleaning), place a good layer of peppers and onions and heavily salt and ground mill pepper, then add another layer of the same until done. Now pour the evoo over the top, add salt and pepper, and place in a preheated 350° oven for 40 minutes, stirring on occasion.

In another baking tray with foil, sprinkle some evoo and lightly salt and pepper. Take your links and, with a fork, poke holes from top to bottom every ¼ inch on two sides (this lets the water out of the links and prevents the links from bursting). Place in oven along pepper tray and cook for 10 minutes. Turn them and cook for an additional 10 minutes. Then remove and thinly slice each link with a sharp charade knife and fork. Take sliced sausages and place them back in the pan to mix with all of the juices. Pour all into your pepper tray and mix well, and put back in the oven until done. Remove tray, give a good stir, cover for 10 minutes on the stovetop, and let rest. Now with a good Italian crusted bread, cut a section of your choice, make a pocket, stuff with your sausage, peppers, and onion, and eat a little piece of heaven!

FRANK'S STUFFED BRACIOLE

(Stuffed Meat Rolls)

Ingredients:
3 pounds beef, bottom round, preferably long in length
4 hardboiled eggs, peeled and chopped
6 cloves fresh peeled and chopped garlic
½ cup slightly toasted pine nuts, chopped
½ cup fresh chopped Italian flat-leaf parsley
1 cup fresh grated Parmigiano-Reggiano cheese
12 thin slices imported Italian Prosciutto Di Parma (a must)
3 cups dry, old, crusty Italian bread, cubed into ¼-inch pieces
1 cup whole milk or half-and-half cream
Kosher salt and fresh-ground mill pepper
12 thin slices provolone cheese
6-8 oz Mascarpone Italian cream cheese
6 tablespoons Italian extra virgin olive oil (evoo)
Butcher twine or toothpicks
3 cups homemade sauce (see my sauce recipe) or a good store brand
1 pound fresh shredded mozzarella

Directions:
In a bowl, add your milk and cubed bread and soak for 30 minutes Now take your bottom round and carefully trim and thinly slice with a sharp knife into long ¼-inch strips until finished (you can have your butcher do this act for you). Lay them on a large tray. Now take each slice of meat, place between two layers of clear wrap, and pound them carefully, not broken into a flatter surface.

Take and drain your soaked bread, squeezing most of the milk out. Place into a large bowl. Add the eggs, garlic, parsley, nuts, grated cheese, and the Italian cream cheese, along with light salt and pepper and 2 tablespoons of evoo, and mix all together well.

Take a large baking dish lined with nonstick foil and brush on evoo, salt, and pepper, then start preparing the braciole. Take each flattened strip, lay on a slice of the provolone cheese and a slice of prosciutto, and spoon in a good amount of your stuffing from your bowl at the top of your strip. Carefully roll over and over, creating a little log. Now you either use the butcher twine to tie ends or stick a toothpick straight through the two ends. Either way, you have a complete braciole. Take your baking tray and lay your braciole log on it, spaced apart. Now it's time to brown your bracioles in a sauté pan on medium heat. Add 4 tablespoons of evoo. When hot, carefully start adding your bracioles with tongs so as not to burn yourself, and turn each in the pan until it becomes a light brown (please do not let them burn). They should only cook for a minute or two. Once browned, place back on the baking tray with a very light coat of salt and pepper, and pour over your homemade sauce. Place in a preheated oven at 375° and cook for 20 minutes, then remove, spread the mozzarella all over, and put back in the oven for 20-30 minutes until the mozzarella is crusty.

Note: You can also just brown your bracioles in a large Dutch oven with 4 tablespoons of evoo until lightly brown. After all are browned, pour in 6-8 cups of your homemade sauce and put on high heat, bringing them to a boil, then down to a simmer. Add all of your bracioles to the sauce and cover with a wooden spoon between the pot and the lid (for venting). Simmer for 4 hours.

Either way you choose, they're just delicious. Well, enjoy!

MY FAMOUS HOMEMADE TOMATO SAUCE

Ingredients:

6 28-oz cans San Marzano whole peeled tomatoes with basil leaf (best of the best)

1 large sweet white onion, chopped

5 cloves fresh minced garlic

½ cup sugar

1 to 2 cups good Italian red wine

4 basil leaves

Kosher salt and fresh-ground mill pepper

6 tablespoons Italian extra virgin olive oil (evoo)

⅛ teaspoon red pepper flakes (add more if you like it hotter)

Directions:

In a large Dutch oven pot, add evoo on medium heat. Once hot, add onion and modestly salt and pepper. Cook down until it is a little translucent. Add garlic, along with the red pepper flakes (do not burn the garlic. If so start over). Garlic should cook for two minutes. Quickly pour in each can of tomatoes and give it a quick stir. With a long-handled chopper, insert it into the pot and chop all of the tomatoes until they are a smooth, creamy texture. Now add your sugar, wine, salt, and pepper, and give it a good long stir. When it starts to boil, stir for 15 seconds and taste. If needed, add salt, pepper, wine, or sugar. It's up to your taste buds. Once that is done, turn down to simmer, cover with the lid with a wooden spoon in between the pot and the lid, and let cook for 4 hours or longer. Every half-hour, uncover and give it a good stir. When time is up, you'll have a delicious sauce for your pasta and other recipes. Enjoy!

STEAK ALLA PIZZAIOLA MIO

(My Way)

Ingredients:
4 thick New York strip steaks, 1 ¼ inches thick, trimmed
2 cans San Marzano crushed tomatoes
½ teaspoon red pepper flakes (more if you like it hot)
5 cloves fresh chopped garlic
3 peppers (1 red, 1 yellow, 1 green), chopped into small pieces with no seeds
2 cup fresh mushrooms, sliced thin (your choice of type)
Kosher salt and fresh-ground mill pepper
8 tablespoons Italian extra virgin olive oil (evoo)
1 cup good Italian red wine

Directions:
Take your steaks out until they are room temperature. In a large Dutch oven or extra-large sauté pan (big enough to fit your steaks and condiments), add 5 tablespoons of evoo on medium heat. Then add garlic and red pepper flakes. Cook for 2 minutes, careful not to burn. Add the peppers, mushrooms, cans of tomatoes, and wine. When it comes to a boil, lower to a simmer and start cooking your steaks. In a large skillet on high heat, coat with 2 tablespoons of evoo and set in your steak carefully. Remember, when there is hot oil, use cooking tongs. Cook on each side for 2½ minutes. Now remove and place inside your pizzaiola sauce that you have created. Stir mixture over the steaks and let cook for 1-2 hours or until meat is fork tender. This is a hearty and tasty dish. Enjoy!

OSO BUCCO

(Braised Veal Shank)

Ingredients:
4 to 6 veal shanks, about 3 to 4 inches each
½ stick salted butter
6 tablespoons Italian extra virgin olive oil (evoo)
½ cup fresh celery stalks, cleaned and chopped
½ cup fresh carrots, cleaned and chopped
1 large white sweet onion, chopped
1½ cups fresh chopped Italian flat-leaf parsley
1½ cups good Italian red wine
1 can Italian tomato paste
Kosher salt and fresh-ground mill pepper

Directions:
In a deep-sided sauté pan on medium heat, add the evoo and butter. Once melted, place your veal shanks in and brown both sides, then remove, place on a tray, and cover with foil. In the same pan, on medium heat add the onion, carrots, paste, salt, and pepper. Lightly cover with lid on and cook for 12-15 minutes or until carrots are fork tender. Now add the wine and, with a wooden spoon, stir and scrape the bottom of the pan for all stuck-on ingredients. After a good stir, add in the browned shanks on low heat, stirring occasionally. Cook for 40 minutes covered. If sauce looks a little dry, just add ½ cup of water, then in 2 minutes stir and taste for salt and pepper. Add if needed. Cover until everything is fork tender. Then remove and let sit for 5 minutes. Plate and serve over rice or small shelled pasta or just as is. Either way, it's great. Don't forget the Italian bread for dipping!

MY HOMEMADE POTATO WEDGES

Ingredients:
6 whole baking potatoes, washed and dried
3½ cups Italian extra virgin olive oil (evoo)
Sea salt and fresh-ground mill pepper
1 cup all-purpose flour

Directions:
Place each potato on a baking tray and, with a fork, poke holes all over each one. Now pour evoo over each, along with salt and pepper, and turn them over and do same to the other side. Now in a preheated oven on 425°, place your tray for 25-30 minutes, then remove it and leave it standing on the stovetop to cool down for 20 minutes or when you are able to handle it without burning yourself. Slice each into wedges, first in half, then quarters. In a bowl, add your flour and place in each wedge, coating them. Place in a deep fryer with evoo and fry until brown and crusty. Place on a paper towel tray. Add salt and pepper to taste and serve.

It's a delicious type of potato. Enjoy!

POLLO ALLA CACCIATORE

(Chicken Hunter Style)

Ingredients:

16 pieces chicken (thighs, legs, and wings—your combo choice), cleaned and trimmed of all fat and skin

2 cups Portobello mushrooms, brushed clean and thinly sliced

3 cups long-grain rice

2 containers 32-oz College Inn culinary broth (white wine and herb)

1 stick salted butter

⅓ cup Italian extra virgin olive oil (evoo)

3 fresh carrots, cleaned and chopped

3 fresh celery stalks, cleaned and chopped

2 fresh peppers (1 red and 1 yellow), cleaned and thinly sliced with no seeds

1 large white sweet peeled onion, thinly sliced

1 can Italian tomato paste

4 tablespoons fresh chopped Italian flat-leaf parsley

1 tablespoon oregano

1 tablespoon rosemary

3 cups good Italian red or white wine, your choice

Kosher salt and fresh-ground pepper

Directions:

In a large Dutch oven pot on medium heat, add evoo. With cooking tongs, carefully add chicken pieces. Do not crowd the pan. Let them brown on both sides. When all is finished, remove and place in a bowl with some paper towels. Quickly add the tomato paste in the same pot and stir in a little circle. Add the onions, carrots, and celery, and stir. Add salt and pepper modestly, and add wine. With the wooden spoon with which you are already stirring, scrape the bottom to loosen all stuck-on goodies. Now add your browned chicken pieces and bring to a boil, then down to a simmer. Put on low heat, cover with lid, and cook for 60 minutes with an occasional stir until fork tender. Check taste for salt and pepper. Add if needed.

Now in a deep pot, add the broth and butter and bring to a boil. Then add your rice. Stir a few times, cover, and cook for 20-25 minutes on low heat. Then check it. If all is puffy and there is no liquid on top, give it a few stirs and cover. Turn heat off and wait for 7 minutes. Now it is ready to serve.

Place a good bed of rice on an extra-large platter and scoop in your chicken cacciatore that you just created. Enjoy! You will!

POLLO CON PROSCIUTTO A FORNO

(Chicken Baked with Italian Ham)

Ingredients:
8 cleaned and trimmed chicken breasts
½ cup Italian extra virgin olive oil (evoo)
24 fresh picked clean Italian sweet basil leaves
8 thin-sliced Prosciutto Di Parma
½ cup good Italian Marsala wine
1½ cups good Italian light white wine
1½ cups College Inn culinary broth (white wine and herb)
1 stick salted butter, split in half
1½ cups all-purpose flour
⅓ cup fresh grated parmesan cheese
Kosher salt and fresh-ground mill pepper
8-12 slices provolone cheese

Directions:
Take each chicken breast, which is neatly trimmed and equal on both sides, and on a hard surface with a sheet of clear wrap, lay down each. With the flat side of your butcher knife, pound down the breast gently to create a flat surface. Now lay about 3 basil leaves across and a slice of prosciutto, and pound down again, making the prosciutto stick to the breast. In a small tray or flat sheet of foil about 20 inches long, pour the flour, grated cheese, salt, and pepper, and with a fork mix together. Dust each breast carefully on both sides, and lay them on a flour dusty tray until it is time to brown.

Once all are floured, in an extra-large Dutch oven on medium heat add the evoo and a half stick of butter and melt down. Then add your breast prosciutto, side down, and brown both sides for about 3-5 minutes on each side. Now after all are browned (not burned), place them on a platter and cover. Quickly add Marsala wine, white wine, and broth on high heat to a boil. Scrape the bottom of the Dutch oven and reduce to a little more than a half-level of liquid. In a large deep-sided baking tray, brush all around with evoo and lay on all of the browned breast prosciutto, side up. Carefully pour in the hot sauce that you have created, and layer with the sliced provolone cheese. Thinly slice the butter into pats and lay on top. Place in a 375° preheated oven for 40 minutes. Remove cover with foil, and let stand on stovetop for 10-15 minutes, then scoop and serve. You'll love it!

FLAVORING OLIVE OIL

Please keep in mind when cooking that Italians always use extra virgin olive oil (evoo), which is the first press of the olives. That's the best. It's all pure with no additives.

I only use evoo to cook and fry in all of my recipes. Do not let anyone tell you any differently!

To flavor evoo to your taste, you'll need an oil bottle with a screw cap and your favorite ingredient or ingredients. All you do is fill half of the bottle with your choice of ingredient and the other half with only evoo. Screw down and shake and leave it standing for one week. Shake every once in a while and stand it upside down. Then insert a pouring spout and use. When finished, just start over again.

You can also use a food processor to blend your choice of ingredients and evoo and pour into the bottle, letting it set as above. When ready, start using.

Some examples of ingredients are garlic, parsley, basil, pine nuts, hot peppers, sweet peppers, anchovies, oregano, mint, lemon rinds, onion, rosemary, dill, anis seeds (fennel seeds), cloves, bay leaves, thyme, saffron (just a small amount), nutmeg, cinnamon, capers, and many more.

There are all types of combinations you can create and other ingredients I did not mention, so have fun creating your special flavor!

THANKSGIVING TURKEY

Ingredients:
15-20-pound fresh killed turkey
4 whole lemons, sliced in quarters
4 sticks salted butter
Kosher salt and fresh-ground mill pepper
10-15 fresh sprigs thyme
10 fresh sprigs rosemary
10-15 leaves fresh sage
¾ cup Italian extra virgin olive oil (evoo)
2 cups College Inn culinary broth (white wine and herb)

Note:
I like to brine my turkey overnight, so in a large pot (big enough to fit a whole turkey), add ½ cup of salt and ½ cup of sugar. Add water to cover ¼ of the way up the pot and stir until dissolved. Now place the turkey in the sink, remove wrapping, empty out the contents (some come in a bag), rip out any organs that are inside, and discard. Run cold water on the turkey and rinse well. Now place the turkey in the pot, legs up, and add cold water to cover. Add another ½ cup of salt and sugar. Cover with clear wrap and refrigerate overnight. When it's time to cook, place it in the sink and rinse well inside and out. Pat dry with paper towels and discard with the brine water.

Directions:
On large pieces of foil, lay the turkey, breast side up, and with your fingers slice in between skin and meat to separate as much as possible without damaging the skin. Now insert pats of butter and sprigs of thyme, rosemary, and sage under the skin. Insert as many as you can all around. Sit the turkey upright, and heavily salt and pepper the inside cavity. When finished, lay down again and stuff inside cavity with 2 whole sticks of salted butter and the lemons, along with leftover thyme, rosemary, and sage. Now with butcher twine, carefully fold legs together and tie, closing the cavity as much as possible. Now turn the turkey breast up and smear butter all over. Heavily salt and pepper and pour evoo all over. Now on your cooking rack pan, lay the turkey breast side down and repeat the same process with extra evoo and herbs. Pour the broth into the pan. Place in a preheated 325° oven for 90 minutes, then remove from the oven. Carefully turn the turkey breast side up back on the rack and put in the oven for 30 minutes, then carefully baste the turkey with the juices in the bottom of the pan. Now fold a piece of foil like a tent (upside down "V") and lay over the top of the turkey, cooking for another 45 minutes. Remove foil and cook for another 15 minutes (total of 180 minutes) until the top of the turkey is golden brown (careful not to burn the top). Now remove the cover with foil. Let it sit on the stovetop for 15 minutes. Now finally it's time to enjoy a great-tasting, moist turkey. Well, Happy Thanksgiving!

AFFOCATO DESSERT

Ingredients:
1 medium pot good Italian espresso coffee
1 quart good vanilla ice cream

Directions:
Scoop 1-2 scoops of vanilla ice cream into a cup or small bowl to serve. Pour hot espresso coffee on top, halfway up, and then enjoy its refreshing flavor with a small spoon. If you want to be fancy, add an Italian wafer on top.

FRANK'S WAY OF MAKING LEMON GRANITA

(Lemon Ice)

Ingredients:
4 cups spring water
1½ cups sugar
Grated zest of 2 lemons (just the outer rind)
2 cups fresh-squeezed lemon juice, no pits

Directions:
In a medium pot on high heat, add the water and sugar and bring to a boil while stirring to dissolve.

Once it boils, lower to a low simmer for 5 minutes. Now carefully pour it into a large deep-sided baking tray and let cool for 20 minutes. Then while stirring, add lemon juice and zest. Now slowly place in the freezer and check in 20 minutes for ice crystals to form. If formed, gently run a fork across all of the crystals to loosen all and stir with fork. Repeat this process until there is no liquid, just ice crystals. Once all is crystallized, remove and scrape into little serving glasses or cups, and enjoy this refreshment!

E' FAMOUSA INSALATA DI MARE CON LEMONE

(My Famous Seafood Salad with Lemon)

Ingredients:

1 pound fresh medium-size cooked shrimp

1 pound canned or fresh scungilli

1 pound fresh cooked calamari, sliced into little rings

1 pound fresh cooked octopus, chopped into small cubes

Note: All of these fish can easily be cooked in boiling water with salt for only 1½ minutes but no longer because they become tough. Also, you can increase the size of the fish amounts to 2-3 pounds. That is all up to you. Also, you need to increase the ingredients accordingly.

2½ cups small green olives, pitted and chopped

3 cups fresh celery stalks, chopped

1 medium-size jar roasted red peppers, drained and sliced into thin strips

2 cups fresh minced garlic

Sea salt and fresh-ground mill pepper

1 cup of fresh chopped Italian flat-leaf parsley

2 cups Italian extra virgin olive oil (evoo)

4 cups fresh-squeezed lemon juice

Directions:

Have all of your ingredients listed above all around you, and in the center place an extra-wide deep bowl or pot. Now start by placing handfuls of each in fish, celery, olives, garlic, and peppers, and sprinkle evoo all over, along with lemon juice. Repeat this process and stir until everything is in the bowl or pot. Now just carefully toss and stir, adding evoo and lemon juice and heavily salting and peppering while stirring. You can start to eat now, or better yet, cover with clear wrap and refrigerate. Every 2 hours, take it out and stir. In 4 hours or next day, take it out and let it stand for 30 minutes. Give it a good stir and toss and drain most of the liquid out. Pour fresh evoo and lemon juice and stir. Scoop into plates or little bowls and enjoy. This is one of my better creations that I developed, and now it's yours. Enjoy!

MY CLASSIC RAGU' BOLOGNESE

(Bolognaise Sauce)

Ingredients:

1 small rind Parmigano-Reggiano cheese (outer hard shell of the cheese)

2 pounds ground beef, 80/20 mix

1½ pounds ground pork

1 pound ground veal

1 large white sweet onion, minced

4 fresh celery stalks, cleaned and chopped

5 fresh cloves minced garlic

2 cups fresh carrots, cleaned, peeled, and chopped

Kosher salt and fresh-ground mill pepper

5 16-oz cans San Marzano peeled tomatoes (pour into a large bowl and crush finely by hand or blend until it is a small chunky texture)

2 cups good Italian red wine

1 cup Italian extra virgin olive oil (evoo)

1 small can tomato paste

1½ cups half-and-half, milk, or heavy cream (your choice)

¼ tablespoon of red pepper flakes (more if you like it hotter)

6 tablespoons sugar

Directions:

In an extra-large pot or Dutch oven over medium heat, add ½ cup of evoo. When hot, add onions, carrots, celery, salt, and pepper accordingly, along with red pepper flakes, and stir. Cook for 10 minutes. Now add your garlic and cook for 2 minutes while stirring. Now add all of your meats and stir in with the remaining evoo, using a wooden spoon to break down the meats. Once the meat seems crumbly, add in the tomato paste and stir. Then add the tomatoes and heavily salt and pepper. Stir for 1 minute. Add wine and sugar and really stir it well until it comes to a boil. Then turn it down to a simmer and place a wooden spoon across the edge, then covering with the lid (so you create a vent space with the spoon). Add your cheese rind and stir every 30-40 minutes. Taste for salt, pepper, and sugar for bitterness, and cook for 4-6 hours on simmer. Always stir so sauce does not stick to the bottom of the pot. Now all you have to do is boil your favorite pasta and plate and pour over your specially made bolognese sauce. A real treat and hardy meal. Enjoy!

SAUTÉED ESCAROLE

(Sautéed Italian Greens)

Ingredients:

6 large heads (bunch) of Italian escarole (For each head of escarole, you must first slice the bottom layer 1/8 of an inch completely off. Then take by hand each leaf and rinse under cool water, removing any dirt.)

½ cup Italian extra virgin olive oil (evoo)

8 cloves fresh garlic, sliced thin

Kosher salt and pepper

Directions:

In extra-large deep pot, take each of the washed leaves and hand rip into small pieces (it's a long job but well worth it). Place them into the pot and just push down to make more room. Heavily salt 3/4 of a cup; it's no problem, just spread it right on top. After all is done, press down and heavily salt again, then fill with water to the top 2 inches below overflow. Place the pot on medium to high heat and cover, leaving a gap between the pot and the lid with a long wooden spoon. Cook for at least 60 minutes, stirring and carefully tossing bottom to top and top to bottom, keeping an eye on the heat level so it does not overflow. After 60 minutes, feel if the leaves are tender and soft. Turn off heat and place the pot in the sink. Scoop with a large strainer and put in a pasta colander for extra draining. Do not worry about overflow in the colander because 6 heads of escarole reduces to less than ⅓. Now with the colander full of your cooked escarole, with a plate on top gently push down and drain more water/juice. Now empty the pot and add evoo on medium heat. When hot, add garlic and stir for 2 minutes. Now add in your escarole and stir well with the garlic. Sprinkle more evoo as you stir and salt and pepper heavily. Stir all together well (I use the pasta long fork to stir). Empty all into a bowl and start tasting a little bite of heaven.

You also have an option to add 2 cans of drained and washed cannellini beans at the same time you add the garlic. It's up to you, just enjoy!

CONCHIGLIE ALLA CREMA
CON CREMA DI PISELLI

Ingredients:
1 pound pasta shells
1 pound Italian pancetta or good bacon, chopped finely
1 medium-size bag frozen peas, thawed
¼ cup Italian extra virgin olive oil (evoo)
½ stick salted butter
2 large bell peppers (1 red and 1 orange), washed and thinly sliced with no seeds
5 cloves fresh minced garlic
1 tablespoon fresh chopped Italian basil
½ tablespoon oregano
1 cup half-and-half
1 8-oz tube Mascarpone Italian cream cheese
Kosher salt and fresh-ground mill pepper

Directions:
In a large deep-sided sauté pan, add 2 tablespoons of evoo on medium heat. Add the pancetta and cook until almost crispy but not burnt. In a bowl, add the cream and Mascarpone and blend together. After pancetta is done, remove, set aside, and drain. Put the pan back on the heat and add the evoo and butter. Once melted, add the peppers, onion, and garlic, and sauté by stirring. Lightly salt and pepper, along with the peas and herbs, and cook for 18-20 minutes on simmer. Everything should be soft. Now add your cream mixture and pancetta and stir until everything is blended together. Simmer and cover for 8 minutes.

In the meantime, you should have your water boiling to cook the pasta shells. Drain well, pour into a sauté pan, and mix everything together and well. Now shut off the heat, pour into a large serving bowl or right out of the pan, plate, and serve. Delicious!

MIO ARANCINI

(My Stuffed Rice Balls)

Ingredients:
4 cups Italian arborio rice
1½ cups fresh grated Parmigiano-Reggiano cheese
12 oz fresh mozzarella, cubed small or in little ball form
1 container 32-oz College Inn culinary broth (white wine and herb)
2 cups frozen peas, thawed
1 pound ground beef, 80/20 mix
4 fresh eggs
½ cup half-and-half cream
¾ stick salted butter
1½ cups Italian extra virgin olive oil (evoo)
¼ cup fresh minced garlic
1½ cups minced white sweet onion
3 cups Italian seasoned breadcrumbs
2 quarts homemade tomato sauce

Directions:
There are four steps:

Step 1: In a pot, heat up culinary broth. In a large sauté pan, add the ½ cup of evoo and butter on medium heat. Add the half of the onion, cook for 2 minutes, and then add half of the garlic. Cook to a very light shade of brown. Then add the rice and stir all around until the rice turns a different shade. Quickly pour in one ladle of hot broth at a time, stirring until the rice is covered with broth, and stir and bring to a low boil. Then bring it down to a simmer, cover, and cook for 25 minutes. In the last few minutes, stir in ½ cup of cheese, then shut off the heat and let it cool down (1 hour) so you will be able to handle the rice.

Step 2: In a large sauté pan, add 2 tablespoons of evoo, the remaining onions. and the remaining garlic. Cook for 2 minutes. Now add the beef and a moderate amount of salt and pepper. Cook until browned to a light color. Now add the peas and ½ quart of your homemade sauce. Heat on simmer with the lid for 20 minutes, cooking off all moisture. When a light and solid consistency is reached, then let cool down as in Step 1.
Step 3: Take your rice mixture and pour into a large bowl, adding 2 eggs and the cheese, mixing all together with your hands. Once the mixture is formed, scoop a medium amount of mixture into a ball (tennis ball size), then with your thumb, press into the center of the ball and create a pocket. Insert some of the mozzarella (cube or ball) and a spoonful of your beef. Add peas and sauce and close. Place on a sheet of nonstick foil. After all is complete, go to Step 4.

Step 4: In a deep-sided small pan, add 2 eggs and half-and-half and whisk to smooth. Lightly salt and pepper and whisk. In another same type of pan, spread the breadcrumbs.

In a large skillet, add 1 cup of evoo on medium heat.

Now take each rice ball that you created and roll into the egg bath, then into the breadcrumbs, and finally into the skillet (careful not to burn yourself). Gently roll them around a few at a time until browned. Place on a large tray with paper towels or a drain screen and let cool off, and then you'll bite into a delicious treat. Enjoy!

COZZE ALI-AROMI

(Clams with Wine and Garlic Sauce)

Ingredients:
3-4 pounds fresh middle or littleneck clams
½ cup oatmeal
½ cup salt
½ cup Italian extra virgin olive oil (evoo)
7 cloves fresh chopped garlic
½ cup fresh chopped Italian flat-leaf parsley
¼ teaspoon red pepper flakes (more if you like it hotter)
3 cups good Italian light white wine

Directions:
Rinse and scrub the clams. Place them in ice water with ½ cup of oatmeal and ½ cup of salt, then make sure they are well rinsed when ready to cook. In a large deep-sided sauté/skillet pan and lid on medium heat, add the evoo. Once hot, add the pepper flakes and garlic and sauté for 2 minutes (not burning garlic. If so start over). Now add the clams and wine. Give it a good stir and cover it with the lid for 7-10 minutes or until the clams are all open. (Remember to discard any unopened clams.) Once open, sprinkle the parsley over all, cover, and shut off heat. 30 seconds later, pour all into a large bowl and serve, scooping clams and sauce into little serving bowls, then eat and dip with good crusty Italian bread. Enjoy!

BRANZIO CON OLIVE' A FORNO

(Sea Bass Baked with Olives)

Ingredients:
8 fresh sea bass fillets (you can use another type of similar fish)
1 cup good Italian light wine
1 cup fresh-squeezed lemon juice
½ cup Italian extra virgin olive oil (evoo)
1 cup sliced calamata olives
3 cups fresh grape or cherry tomatoes, sliced
6 cloves fresh thin-sliced garlic
2 teaspoons oregano
Sea salt and fresh-ground mill pepper

Directions:
In a large roasting pan lined with nonstick foil, brush bottom with evoo and lay each fillet side by side. In a large bowl, pour in the wine, lemon juice, the remaining evoo, and calamata olives. Add the sliced tomatoes and the salt and pepper to taste, along with the garlic and oregano, and stir mixture. Now pour the mixture into the roasting pan with your fillets, covering all with foil, and place in the preheated 375° oven for 10 minutes. Now remove the foil cover and roast for another 10 minutes or until the sea bass is tender to touch by fork. Remove from oven, plate, and serve, pouring sauce over each fillet, and just enjoy!

Note: You may use more than one roasting pan if all does not fit.

BRUSCHETTA DI MOZZARELLA
CON POMODORO

(Italian Toast with Mozzarella, Sliced Tomatoes, and Sauce)

Ingredients:

6 fresh ripe tomatoes, chopped in a bowl

6 tablespoons fresh chopped Italian sweet basil leaves

12 slices fresh crusted Italian bread, about 1 inch thin

16 oz fresh mozzarella cheese, diced small

6 tablespoons Italian extra virgin olive oil (evoo)

2 teaspoons oregano

1 small jar capers, rinsed and drained

¼ cup good aged Italian balsamic vinegar

¼ or ½ cup fresh minced garlic (your choice)

1 tablespoon sea salt

2 tablespoons fresh-ground mill pepper

Directions:

In a large bowl, add your tomatoes with juices, mozzarella, oregano, evoo, balsamic vinegar, and salt and pepper, and stir well. Let sit and cover with clear wrap. Put in the refrigerator for 20-30 minutes. In the meantime, on a grill pan on medium heat brush each slice of bread with evoo and toast on grill pan on both sides. Place them on a large serving platter. Take your mixture and stir for 1 minute, then scoop the mixture on each side of toasted bread (you may add more salt, pepper, and balsamic vinegar if you like). Now this a real treat. You'll love it. Enjoy!

FRANK'S SAUTÉED MUSHROOMS

Ingredients:
4 cups fresh thin-sliced mushrooms (your choice; I use Portobello)
5 tablespoons Italian extra virgin olive oil (evoo)
Kosher salt and fresh-ground mill pepper
¼ cup red wine vinegar or good Italian red wine
6 cloves fresh thin-sliced garlic

Directions:
In an extra-large nonstick sauté pan on medium heat, add evoo and garlic, cook for 2 minutes (careful not to burn garlic. If so start over), and stir. Then add in the mushrooms and stir, along with vinegar or wine. Add salt and pepper to taste and let cook with cover lid until the mushrooms are soft to touch and liquid has reduced, which should be about 10-12 minutes. Then just plate and enjoy. This is a good side dish with a steak and great bottle of Italian red wine. Sounds so good. Enjoy!

Note: This recipe can also be used with fresh spinach in place of the mushrooms (2 bags of 12-oz fresh spinach). In this recipe, you get two for the price of one!

SCALLOPINE DI VITELLO

(Veal Scallopine)

Ingredients:

2 pounds fresh veal cutlet, thinly sliced to about ½ inch each (about 10 fillets)

1 cup good Italian red wine

½ cup fresh-squeezed lemon juice, strained

¾ cup Italian extra virgin olive oil (evoo)

½ cup all-purpose flour

1 tablespoon kosher salt

1 tablespoon fresh-ground mill pepper

1 cup fresh minced sweet onion

¼ teaspoon paprika

3 tablespoons fresh minced garlic

2 tablespoons fresh chopped Italian flat-leaf parsley

2½ cups fresh thin-sliced mushrooms (your choice; I use Portobello)

½ stick salted butter

Directions:

Place each slice of veal fillet between a layer of clear wrap and pound gently to spread the meat thinner, but be careful not to break (about 1/4 inch thick). Then in a mixing tray, add the flour, salt, pepper, and paprika, and mix well with a fork. Now coat each veal fillet with the mixture and dust off excess. Then place it in a preheated sauté pan on medium heat with evoo and lightly brown both sides (very lightly). Place on a platter with paper towels to drain any excess oil and cover with foil. When done, add evoo if needed, then add butter and onions and cook for 2 minutes. Add garlic and stir for 1 minute, and then add the mushrooms. Place the lid on top and cook until they are tender (about 8 minutes). Then add your wine and lemon juice. Quickly place in all of your fillets and sprinkle with the parsley. Check for salt and pepper and add if needed. Pour sauce over the fillets, cover, and cook for 7 minutes. Plate and serve. Another enjoyable dish. Do not forget the Italian bread. It's a must for dipping!

GAMBERETTI ALLA POLPETTINE

(Fried Shrimp Balls)

Ingredients:
2 pounds fresh medium-size shrimp, peeled, deveined, and chopped
½ cup Italian extra virgin olive oil (evoo)
½ stick salted butter
1 cup fresh minced sweet white onion
1 cup fresh celery stalks, cleaned and chopped
¼ cup fresh chopped Italian flat-leaf parsley
½ cup fresh chopped Italian sweet basil
1 teaspoon paprika
4 fresh eggs
3 cups Italian seasoned breadcrumbs
3 tablespoons half-and-half
Kosher salt and fresh-ground mill pepper

Directions:
In a large sauté pan/skillet, add 3 tablespoons of evoo and butter on medium heat. Once melted, add the onions and celery and cook until tender, about 5-6 minutes. Now add in your shrimp and sauté all for 2 minutes, then pour everything into a bowl and stir. Add the paprika and basil. Break 2 eggs and, with a wooden spoon, mix and stir in 2 cups of breadcrumbs. Let cool down. Once ready, pour a sprinkle of evoo into your hands and scoop a little amount of the mixture. Roll into little ping-pong-size balls, placing them on a nonstick sheet of foil. Now put it into two separated bowls, one with 2 eggs and half-and-half (the family secret). Beat well. In the other bowl, pour the remaining breadcrumbs. Now take each shrimp ball, roll into egg, and then put in the breadcrumbs and into a large sauté/skillet pan. Add all of the evoo and carefully brown each shrimp ball (not to burn) all around. Then place them on a platter with paper towels to drain the excess oil. Now you can serve using your homemade sauce or a good vinaigrette dressing in a leafy salad. Either way, enjoy!

CALAMARI FRITTI ALLA SALSA MIO

(Fried Calamari with My Sauce)

Ingredients:
2½ pounds fresh calamari, cleaned and sliced into ¼-inch rings
2 cups Italian extra virgin olive oil (evoo)
½ cup whole milk or half-and-half cream
1/4 cup fresh minced garlic
1½ cups fresh grated Pecorino-Romano cheese
½ cup fresh minced Italian flat-leaf parsley
3 cups Italian seasoned breadcrumbs
1 teaspoon sea salt
1 teaspoon fresh-ground mill pepper
5-6 eggs

Directions:
In a large bowl, beat 2-3 eggs, along with milk or cream, until frothy. In another bowl, add the ½ cup of evoo, parsley, garlic, 1 1/2 cups of breadcrumbs, grated cheese, salt, and pepper, and mix well with a wooden spoon. Place the bowls side by side, egg mix first, and take a scoop of calamari with a vented large spoon and soak well. Then place them in the breadcrumb mixture and mix well, carefully dusting off excess. Place in a deep-sided sauté pan/skillet on medium heat with the remaining evoo or use a deep fryer and cook until golden brown. Then place them on a tray or platter with paper towels to drain the excess oil.

Now to make the sauce to dip in:

1 cup Italian extra virgin olive oil (evoo)
½ cup fresh minced garlic
1 teaspoon sugar
1 teaspoon oregano
2 tablespoons fresh minced Italian sweet basil
1 teaspoon sea salt
1 teaspoon fresh-ground mill pepper
3 egg yolks, in a small cup or bowl (optional)
5 tablespoons fresh-squeezed lemon juice, strained
1 teaspoon chopped thyme
2 tablespoons Dijon mustard
½ teaspoon hot sauce

Place all of the above ingredients in a blender on low speed until it's creamy. Pour out and dip your hot fried calamari, and enjoy!

FRANK'S STUFFED BAKED SEA TROUT

Ingredients:

4-6 fresh sea trout, about 1/2-3/4 pounds each, cleaned and gutted (cut off all fins, not the heads)

1 cup fresh sweet white onion, chopped

1 cup fresh celery stalks, cleaned and chopped

½ cup fresh minced garlic

½ cup fresh chopped Italian flat-leaf parsley

½ cup fresh chopped sage

3½ cups Italian seasoned breadcrumbs

¾ cup toasted and chopped pine nuts

½ cup grated Perorino-Romano cheese

3 eggs

4 tablespoons fresh chopped Italian sweet basil

Sea salt and fresh-ground mill pepper

½ cup Italian extra virgin olive oil (evoo)

1½ cups good Italian wine

Directions:

On a large baking tray lined with heavy-duty nonstick foil, place each trout brushed with evoo on the tray side by side. Now in a large nonstick sauté pan on medium heat, add the remaining evoo. Add the onions and celery and sauté for 2 minutes, then add garlic and sauté for 1 minute. Once all seems cooked and not burnt, pour into a large bowl, along with the breadcrumbs, parsley, sage, pine nuts, cheese, moderate salt and pepper, and ½ cup of wine. Mix well with a wooden spoon. With one hand, carefully lift open the cavity of the trout and, with a spoon, stuff it well as much as possible. If there is any remaining stuffing, just fill in the spaces and pour in the wine all around but not on the fish. Place in a preheated 375° oven with a foil cover and cook for 30 minutes. In 15 minutes, remove the foil cover and finish cooking until the fish is very fork tender. Remove and carefully scoop each whole trout with the juices onto a serving plate and enjoy!

FRANK'S LOVABLE MEATBALLS

Ingredients:
2 pounds fresh-ground beef, 80/20 mix
1½ pounds fresh-ground pork
1 pound fresh-ground veal
1 pound fresh-ground lean sirloin
3 cups Italian seasoned breadcrumbs
1 pint half-and-half cream
1 cup fresh grated Pecorino-Romano cheese
¼ cup fresh minced garlic
1 cup fresh chopped Italian flat-leaf parsley
4 fresh eggs
2 tablespoons kosher salt
2½ tablespoons fresh-ground mill pepper
16 oz fresh shredded mozzarella
1½ cups Italian extra virgin olive oil (evoo)

Directions:
In small bowl, add the breadcrumbs and half-and-half and mix well until all is moist. Place it to the side. Do not make it too wet. If so, add a little more breadcrumbs. Leave all the meats out until it is room temperature, then in a super-large metal bowl, add all of the meats and hand mix together well. Now flatten out the meats to create a center for ingredients. Add in the garlic, parsley, salt, and pepper, and break in the eggs (remove any shells that fall in). Add the grated cheese and evoo and the bowl of moist breadcrumbs, and hand mix together (it's a little messy, but you are cooking Italian style). Now flatten and create a center. Add the shredded mozzarella and mix together by hand again. In a large tray lined with nonstick foil and brushed with evoo, start hand rolling a scoop of meatball mixture in a desired-size ball. (I roll them to a little less than a tennis ball size.)

Lay them side by side in the pan. Place the completed tray in a preheated 350° oven for no longer than 6 minutes, and turn over once during baking. Remove and eat, or the secret is to place them carefully in a large pot of homemade sauce and cook on simmer for 3 hours, then eat and enjoy with your favorite pasta or good Ital-ian crusty bread. Yummy good! Enjoy!

SALSICCIA AL FORNO MIO

(Sausage Baked My Way)

Ingredients:
3 pounds or more fresh linked hot or sweet Italian sausage (or both)
5 tablespoons kosher salt
4 tablespoons fresh-ground mill pepper
¼ cup Italian extra virgin olive oil (evoo)

Directions:
On a large baking tray to fill all of the links, line with nonstick foil, brush with a few tablespoons of evoo, and lightly salt and pepper. Now take each sausage link and, with a fork, poke holes from top to bottom about 1/4 inch apart on all sides, then lay them on the baking tray. Sprinkle with evoo and the remaining salt and pepper over all. Place in a preheated 350° oven and cook for 30 minutes, turning once during cooking. Then look and see that it is browned and juicy and remove. Now you can eat as is or add to your homemade sauce (if so, add all of the juices) or just on a good piece of Italian bread. Either way, you will enjoy it!

FRANK'S FAMOUS PASTA AL FORNO

(My Famous Baked Pasta)

Note: This recipe has been a family secret handed down for years.

Ingredients:
1½ pounds fresh-ground beef, 80/20 mix
1 pound fresh-ground pork
1 pound fresh-ground veal
1 large white sweet onion, diced
4 fresh celery stalks, cleaned and diced
1½ cups fresh carrots, cleaned and diced
5 cloves fresh minced garlic
1½ cups good red wine
½ can Italian tomato paste
4 16-oz cans San Marzano peeled tomatoes, hand crushed or by blender, in a bowl with juices
¾ cup Italian extra virgin olive oil (evoo)
8 hardboiled eggs, without shells and thinly sliced
3 16-oz packages fresh shredded mozzarella
2 pounds spaghetti in a box or bag
Kosher salt and fresh-ground mill pepper
¼ cup sugar

Directions:
All of the meats should be left out until they are room temperature.

Step 1: In a large pasta pot with strainer, add water ¾ of the way and bring to a boil. Once it boils, add 4 tablespoons of salt.

Step 2: In a medium-size Dutch oven pot on medium heat, add 6 tablespoons of evoo and tomato paste. Stir and sauté the onions, celery, and carrots for 4-5 minutes, then add the garlic and sauté for 1 more minute. Stir with a wooden spoon and moderately salt and pepper (you can add some red pepper flakes if you like). Now add all of the meats and the remaining evoo and stir well. Break down your meats, then add the wine. Mix well along with the sugar. Now add the tomatoes and juices and the salt and pepper to taste, and stir, bringing it to a boil. Then turn the heat down to a simmer and cook for 3 hours with occasional stirring so the sauce does not stick to the bottom of the pot. Place the wooden spoon between the pot and the lid for the venting. Once done, just let it sit on the stovetop for a few hours. This will thicken the sauce.

Now that you feel ready to create my Pasta Al Forno, let's start Step 1 and boil the pasta water. When boiling, add salt and pasta, stirring every few minutes so the pasta does not stick. Cook and stir for 7 minutes and then drain well in an extra-large bowl. Add 2-3 ladles of your sauce, then pour half of the cooked pasta in the bowl and add 4 ladles of the sauce. Pour in the remaining pasta and 3 more ladles of sauce, and mix by tossing it around in the bowl.

Now in a medium deep-sided disposable aluminum tray, pour 5 ladles of sauce and spread it all around, then add a good layer of pasta and a good layer of sauce. Spread a layer of mozzarella and another good layer of pasta and sauce, then mozzarella again before the last layer of pasta and sauce with the mozzarella. Place a layer of the sliced hardboiled eggs, then the last layer. Now put a strong tray under your tray of Pasta Al Forno because of its weight. Place in a preheated oven at 350° for 45 minutes or until the top mozzarella layer is crusty around the edges and lightly bubbling. Remove and cover with a sheet of foil. Place on the stove, then let sit for 1 hour. Then scoop out little sections onto plates and eat. Some prefer extra sauce, and feel free to sprinkle the grated cheese any way you like. Just eat and really enjoy! This is a classic secret!

MY FAMOUS HOMEMADE MEATLOAF

Ingredients:
1 pound fresh-ground beef, 80/20 mix
½ pound fresh-ground pork
½ pound fresh-ground veal
½ pound fresh-ground lean sirloin
½ cup fresh grated Pecrino-Romano cheese
2 cups Italian seasoned breadcrumbs
½ pint half-and-half
4 cloves fresh minced garlic
½ cup fresh chopped Italian flat-leaf parsley
¾ cup Italian extra virgin olive oil (evoo)
3 fresh eggs
2 tablespoons kosher salt
2 tablespoons fresh-ground mill pepper
16 oz fresh shredded mozzarella
1 container 32-oz of College Inn culinary broth (white wine and herb)
1 20-oz or so bag frozen corn
1 20-oz or so bag frozen peas
¼ stick salted butter

Directions:
Leave all meats out until they are room temperature. Put the breadcrumbs in a bowl, add cream, and mix well.

In an extra-large metal bowl, place in all of the meats and hand mix together. Then flatten them to create a center for the ingredients, adding grated cheese, garlic, parsley, evoo, eggs (remove any shells), salt and pepper, and mixed breadcrumbs. Hand mix again until all is blended well (remember, you're cooking Italian, so your hands are a great tool). Flatten and add the shredded mozzarella, then mix again, creating a giant loaf or two small loaves. (I'm Italian, so I like them big.) Now in a large deep-sided baking dish or tray lined with nonstick foil, lay your meatloaf creation in the center. Sprinkle a little evoo over all and add the frozen peas and corn all around but not on top. Then pour the culinary broth in around the sides. Place in a preheated 375° oven for 45 minutes. After 30 minutes, add thin slices of butter on top of the loaf, and when it is melted, carefully deep slice across the loaf from one end to the other every 2 inches for an internal browning. For the remaining time, the loaf should have a light brown crust on top. This means it's ready. Remove and rest on the stovetop, cover with foil for 10 minutes, then cut, scoop, and serve, adding some cooked sauce with the peas and corn. This is truly a good-tasting dish. Well, enjoy!

Pre Cooked Pasta A Forno

Frank's Pese Al Lemone A Forno

Zuppz Di Vongole Siciliano

Cooked Pasta A Forno

Veal chop Polenta

Tutta A' Frittata

Pre cooked meat balls

Pork ribs cooking

Pre cooked peppers and onions

Salsiccia Al Forno Mio

My Italian sausages with peppers and onions

My Italian sausage and pepper and onion sandwich

My Meat sauce with meatballs, ribs and sausage

Frank's famous lemon chicken

Flavored rice

Oso bucco my way

My Famous Homemade Meatloaf

Pasta with my meat sauce

Frank's creamy mashed potatoes

Sautéed Escarole

Sautéed hot peppers

Plate of pasta with my sauce

Pre Cooked chicken with eggplant, prosciutto, cheese and sauce

Stuffed mushroom caps

Stuffed eggplant pie

Bacon wrapped sea scallops

Stuffed peppers

My Insalata Di pomodore E' Cipolle

Pasta Carbonta

Tray of eggplant parm my way

My homemade tomato sauce

Italian curly pasta with my sauce

Oven roasted whole chicken and homemade potatoes

My homemade antipasta

Mozzarella, tomato, basil with EVOO and balsamic vinegar, salt and pepper

My Famous cooked Pasta Al Forno